7 Steps to A Magnetic Personality

Prem P. Bhalla

GOODWILL PUBLISHING HOUSE®
B-3 RATTAN JYOTI, 18 RAJENDRA PLACE
NEW DELHI-110008 (INDIA)

Published by
GOODWILL PUBLISHING HOUSE®
B-3 Rattan Jyoti, 18 Rajendra Place
New Delhi-110008 (INDIA)
Tel. : 25750801, 25820556
Fax : 91-11-25764396
e-mail : goodwillpub@vsnl.net
website : www.goodwillpublishinghouse.com

Printed at :
Kumar Offset, Delhi

Contents

Preface

Step 1. A Magnetic Personality 1

Step 2. Essentials of Personal Magnetism 22

Step 3. Physical Health 43

Step 4. Emotional Health 63

Step 5. Relationships 85

Step 6. Etiquette and Manners 110

Step 7. Developing Personal Magnetism 138

Preface

People are known and accepted in society on the basis of the image they project in everyday life. To impress others most people go to great lengths to dress to attract attention, to build and live in homes that may not necessarily reflect the happiness they derive from them. They acquire status symbols like luxury cars, original paintings and pieces of art that single them out amongst others. However, the satisfaction one derives from these possessions is temporary.

What kind of an image do you project of yourself? It is likely that different people have varied opinion about you. Your wife and the family may have one impression about you and the friends quite another. It is possible that people in general will have yet another opinion about you. In addition, you may think very differently about yourself, thus creating many separate images of yourself.

Most people are content as they are. However, a person who wants to get ahead in life strives to make the best of the gifts of nature. He or she is conscientious, honest and straightforward, and strives to remove the parallax between the several images that one casts in everyday life. Such people learn to create harmony between actions and the image that they reflect.

Change is an integral part of our life. Each day, every hour and every minute, our life is undergoing a change.

Whether it is for better or for worse depends upon how a person takes control of life. Since no two people have the same inherited characteristics, each one reacts differently, and grows up to be an individual personality, unique in every way.

This book aims at taking you step by step into the intricacies of developing a magnetic personality. Charles Schwab rightly said, "Personality is to a man what perfume is to a flower." The book will help you understand the qualities that contribute to the development of the personality. It will also guide you to know yourself and the people around you better. Through effort and perseverance you can add new dimensions to your life through personal magnetism.

— Prem P. Bhalla

A Magnetic Personality

Everyone desires to have a magnetic personality. However, everyone is not fortunate to possess the desirable qualities that contribute to make one attractive. People wonder if these qualities are a gift of God passed on at the time of birth, or can they be acquired through learning and effort? Are there any constraints to learning to develop a magnetic personality? Can everyone acquire these qualities? What are the basic essentials? How and when can a person acquire them? These questions, and many more, continue to confuse aspiring young people who set out to develop personal magnetism with an aim to do great things in life.

People are known by the image they project. Everyone desires to project a positive image of one's personality, but it does not always happen that way. Several factors influence the image and the personality. One will need to know and understand these in greater detail.

The word: magnet immediately conjures an image of an iron bar attracting similar items and objects. The word: magnetic describes the quality of attraction. Used in conjunction with the word: personality, one immediately visualises a person who is both pleasing and attractive. That is the kind of person everyone desires to be. Let us proceed step by step how an ordinary person can develop the qualities that lead to a magnetic personality.

WHERE SHOULD ONE BEGIN?

Every aspiring young person seeks the answer to this question. Wherever can one begin? The answer lies in yet another question. Can one begin from any other place than where one is today? No, one cannot. Just as it is said that a journey of a thousand miles begins with a single step, one begins to develop a magnetic personality from wherever one is today. One needs to begin with a firm determination to bring about changes in life that would help develop the personality.

Some take a vow to change for better. Most people only 'wish' for a change. Wishing is accepting one's inability to acquire what one desires. Wishing aims at seeking it from God, and not through personal effort. That would be inviting failure. Nothing can be achieved without personal effort. If you are not satisfied with what you are today, the effort you would need to make will have to be different. If one were to keep doing the things one has always done, one should not expect the results to be any different from what they have always been. To obtain better results one needs to change what one is doing today. The first step would have to be the acceptance for the need to change.

THE MAGIC OF CHANGE

No progress is possible without an attitude to change for the better. Progress comes from trying new things and making them work. Unfortunately, the vast majority resists change. They desire that the circumstances and the people around them should change. Individually, every person creates a comfort zone and resists getting out of it. Even when a person is motivated to step out of the comfort zone and experience the great potential that is waiting to be tapped, one is only temporarily stirred to action. The efforts are flirtatious and one soon falls back to what one is used to, rationalizing the lack of action.

This attitude is not difficult to understand. Hidden within change is an air of uncertainty. This uncertainty is bound to frighten everyone. This fear keeps people away from change. People are afraid to lose what they have in lieu of what they anticipate in uncertainty. To face this fear you will need to act brave, and step out boldly to face new circumstances. Greater things are not too far away.

Another reason that makes people resist change is lack of knowledge on how to change. What is expected of them to change the circumstances around them? Will it in anyway affect whatever they are enjoying presently? Will change take them towards progress and development? The answers to these questions lie in getting to know one better. One needs to be aware of the circumstances. One needs to gain knowledge to face the likely situations.

Think it over...

It is not what he has, or even what he does which expresses the worth of a man, but what he is.

— *Amiel*

WHO ARE YOU?

This question may appear odd to most people. However, if a person has to develop the personality, beginning from wherever one is today, it is necessary to know oneself. Everyone would vehemently emphasize that a person knows oneself best. But that is not true. It might be all right from the individual's point of view. When we look at people we find that every individual is 'many persons in one'. An individual's spouse may hold one image of the person; the friends may hold quite another. In the same way the society may look at the individual from yet another perspective. Surprisingly, the individual may have an altogether different image of oneself. With different people looking at you from different angles, and holding a variety of images that you have projected through your actions, the question is which one of these is the real you?

You may say, "I am not what you think I am". How is the other person to know who or what you are? Every person holds an image of another based upon the individual's actions. When a person projects several images, which often happens, one should not be surprised if these are not in harmony with the image one holds of oneself. These multiple images are a result of inconsistent behaviour or actions of an individual. These need to be corrected. The parallax between the different images needs to be removed. This is possible only when an individual understands the need for consistent behaviour to develop a magnetic personality.

KNOW YOURSELF

You are what your basic characteristics, which you inherited from your parents, have made you when they reacted with the circumstances and the environment in which you have grown up. Irrespective of whether you like it or not, the changing circumstances continue to mould individuals and their personalities. Since every individual is born unique the reactions in individuals are likely to be different. Two options are available to everyone. The first is to let the circumstances take you wherever they will. The second is to take control of yourself and mould your life and personality, as you would like it to be. The choice is yours.

Everyone would like to take control of life and mould one's own destiny. This is the more difficult method of the two. It would require discipline and effort. It would require that you know your own strengths and weaknesses. While on one hand you would need to add on to the strengths, on the other hand you will need to get over your weaknesses. The two together will take you towards personal development and success. Our immediate object is to develop a magnetic personality. We will need to understand this better.

PERSONAL MAGNETISM

While the word: personal relates to a person, an individual human being, the word: magnetism is often used to describe the ability to attract and charm people.

In reality, magnetism is a property displayed by magnets, and is produced by the movement of electric charges, which results in objects being attracted or pushed away. Every magnet is said to have a magnetic field, which is the region around a magnet within which the force of magnetism acts.

In Physics, magnetism is described as the phenomena by which materials exert a force to attract or repel other materials. Some of the materials that exhibit magnetic properties include nickel, iron, some steels and magnetite. Although these materials exhibit strong magnetic forces, all materials are influenced to some degree by the presence of a magnetic field.

Going back to childhood lessons in school, the force of magnetism is demonstrated by stroking a piece of iron with a strong magnet resulting in the piece of iron acquiring magnetic qualities. It was explained that the stroking magnet realigns the molecules in the piece of iron. With the molecules arranged in a north-south pattern, the piece of iron develops magnetic qualities.

If it were not for the knowledge of magnetism, it would not have been possible to travel around the world, finding directions accurately with the magnetic compass. The force of magnetism has made it possible to generate electricity and move the wheels of industry around the world. Without our being aware of it, magnets play a crucial part in our everyday life.

What role does the force of magnetism play in the lives of people? Just as the earth is a huge magnet with north and south poles, are individuals also like magnets? When we talk of a person having a magnetic personality, and the ability of the person to attract others, and also goodwill and success, can we say that such a person enjoys a large magnetic field? Individuals who developed personal magnetism to a very high degree are often godlike and illustrated with a halo. Does this halo represent the presence of a vast magnetic field?

A child is not born with personal magnetism. It is not an inherited characteristic. It is developed over a long period. Is the option of developing personal magnetism restricted to a limited few, or can everyone do it? When a person is attracted towards a magnetic personality can he or she feel a distinct force? Why is it that a person feels calm and comfortable in the company of some people, and uncomfortable and oppressed in the company of others? The questioning mind seeks the answers to these questions, and many more.

Think it over...

Do you know what a man is? Are not birth, beauty, good shape, discourse, manhood, learning, gentleness, virtue, youth, liberality, and such like, the spice and salt that season a man?

— *Shakespeare*

HUMAN MAGNETS

Scientists seek proof for everything. In the absence of distinct proof they do not agree that human beings are like magnets. However, just as a magnet can magnetize another piece of iron with its influence, similarly a good person can influence another person. It is an acknowledged fact that in the company of good people one learns good things, and in the presence of bad company one can go astray. It is also agreed that persons with similar temperaments are attracted to each other. For example, in any class one sees that the studious kind form one group, and the mischievous ones form yet another group. Even in social life it is common to see people who consume alcoholic beverages flock together while the teetotalers sit separately. It is difficult to explain how or why it happens.

A common explanation that is offered is that, all human beings are sending out vibrations, both positive and negative. These vibrations emerging from different persons influence each other. They attract and also repel. People who attend community prayers may contribute little to the congregation, yet they come home happier because of the influence of the positive vibrations emerging from the large number of people assembled at one place for prayer.

People travel long distances to visit temples, mosques, churches and gurudwaras. In many of these places of faith and prayer the positive vibrations are very strong because of widespread praying and a powerful deity. Unknown to the visitors these vibrations quietly transform individuals just as though one were in the field of a powerful magnet. The magnetic field of a magnet can be charted. The vibrations in these places can be felt.

Have you ever noticed how the feeling of gaiety abounds everywhere at Diwali or Christmas? Have you experienced the joy when one's country wins a crucial match of international significance to gain eminence? In the same way, have you noticed how the feeling of hatred penetrates through the atmosphere when a mob turns violent over an incident? It is the unseen vibrations emerging from people that influence others for both good and bad. We cannot see them but can feel them.

What is especially important to the common man is that, just like a piece of iron that can be magnetized, humans can also develop magnetism. Through experience mankind has learnt the intricacies of the development of a magnetic personality. We will learn it step by step.

MAGNET THERAPY

Scientists are not convinced about the influence of magnets in treatment of diseases. Some even call it a commercial gimmick. Yet there is a growing group of people who use magnets to correct medical problems in human beings. Millions of people are using magnetic bracelets, necklaces, belts, pillows and mattresses to obtain relief from a variety of problems. While many users claim to experience a marked relief from their problems, scientists who seek reason, logic and proof trash the concept as baseless.

The treatment of diseases with magnets is known as magneto-therapy. Books on the subject are freely available advocating it as an alternate system of healing. Many therapists are practicing it. Magnets in a variety of forms are being manufactured and sold in the market. Even the drinking water treated by placing it on magnets is said to promote good health.

Once again, the questioning mind wants to know what is the truth about magneto-therapy? Does it work? Or is it some form of faith healing? Unfortunately, in the absence of the kind of proofs that scientists demand, it is difficult to explain how magnets affect human beings. At the same time when we see the relief that comes from such treatment, we cannot totally agree that magnet healing is only a kind of faith healing.

We do know that every magnet has a magnetic field. We also know that the materials that come within the magnetic field of a magnet are affected by the magnetic waves. It may not be possible to give definite proofs as desired by scientists, but we do know that vibrations from one person influence another person. Could the magnetic waves from magnets be creating similar kinds of reactions in individuals? Could magnets be altering human functions somewhat like hormones that serve as chemical messengers? In the absence of detailed research it is not possible to convincingly answer the questions. At the same time it would not be right to reject the whole concept altogether. Magnets do influence human behaviour.

THERAPEUTIC USE OF ELECTRICITY

Electricity is known to contribute to the life force. In the field of medicine electric shocks have been known to revive dying persons, and also correct certain states of the mind. It is also used in other spheres of medicine. Taking advantage of the use of electricity, innovative persons came out with 'tractors' that could draw disease and pain out of the body, belts and corsets powered with batteries that could cure a variety of problems and e-meters that were used for mental and physical healing. The use of these contraptions have been opposed and action taken against unscrupulous persons taking advantage of gullible patients.

RELATIONSHIPS AND MAGNETISM

It has been observed that people with similar temperaments flock together. Gradually people gravitate to their own kinds making distinct groups. Even within the groups people develop deeper relationships that exert pressure on each other to conform. Scientists would explain that hormones are responsible for this behaviour. Hormones are chemical messengers and can therefore be identified. Much research has been done on the subject. One can hold them responsible for a lot of human reactions. But how do we explain 'love at first sight'? This could be between a male and a female, but could also be between two persons of the same sex. They may be strongly attracted to each other. What makes it happen?

Touch is a distinct factor that can set reactions in motion. When a young man and woman hold hands their reactions could be due to the sex hormones in action. But how do we explain the pleasure two friends derive when they embrace each other after a long time? It might be easy to explain the bonds between a mother and her child. But what about the pleasure one derives from embracing someone's child? Isn't there a distinct pleasure of touch without the element of sex having to do anything with it? Both enjoy equally. We see it happen everywhere every day.

In some cultures it is customary for the younger persons to touch the feet of elders, teachers and those who are superior in one way or another. It is also explained how this is to be done. It is explained that by touching the feet the person draws good vibrations from the elders. In response, while the person conveys blessings by placing the hands on the head, once again vibrations are exchanged. Such customs have been in use for thousands of years. They are still being practiced. Why? It could be explained that touching of the feet is an exercise in humility.

In response, the touching of the head or the shoulder is giving of a blessing. Is this blind faith, or does the custom have a definite meaning? How does it work?

In the **Mahabharat**, **Vanparv**, Yaksh, protecting the lake, asked Yudhistra to answer his questions before he could be allowed to drink water. One of the questions was, "How can a person become great and powerful?"

Yudhistra responded, "By devotedly touching the feet of the mother and father, teachers and elders and by serving them until they are content to give blessings that make a person great and powerful."

This pertains to a period over 2500 years ago. In the modern context it could be interpreted to mean that a person must be humble and seek good vibrations from the parents, teachers and the elders.

The handshake is a common form of greeting in many cultures. Giving a hug is also used as a greeting. Without being aware of it, are the people not exchanging vibrations? On most occasions it is a pleasant thing to do. In some cases the experience could also be repulsive.

Think it over...

It's beauty that captures your attention; personality, which captures your heart.

—*Anon*

THE HUMAN BODY

Every individual is identified to be the physical body seen by everyone. It is this body that projects an image of an ordinary person or that of a magnetic personality. People go to great lengths to project the best possible image. Everyone wants to know how it can be done better. Before one can do that it would be necessary to understand the human body correctly.

The human body is a master creation. All of science and technology put together cannot create anything close to it. Scientists have tried to unravel the mysteries of the human body to give it a longer lease of life by protecting it from disease and sickness. It has been possible to study the human body in minute detail and very often to correct life-threatening problems. Yet, life and death continue to remain a mystery.

The science of Genetics explains that an individual is born from the union of the sperm from the father and the ovum from the mother. The characteristics of the individual depend upon the genes carried by the sperm and ovum. Since there are millions of sperms carrying a variety of combinations at the time of union with the ovum, which carries the genes from the mother, it is difficult to predict what a child would look like. This makes every individual unique. The sperm and the ovum are known to carry genes of desirable and undesirable characteristics. No control is possible over them. Therefore, one has to be content with the characteristics one is born with.

Science has been able to minutely study different systems like the nervous system, the circulatory system, the digestive system, the loco-motor system and others that constitute the human body, and work in unison, each system supporting the others. All the systems are regulated through the controlling system located in the brain. The ability to see, hear, speak and move about and perform other human functions is also controlled by the brain. When different systems fail to work in harmony sickness creeps in. If attended to in time the body becomes normal again. With time there is a gradual fall in performance of the different systems ultimately resulting in systems failure and death.

Hindu religious texts written over 2500 years ago contend that the human body is a vehicle driven by soul. While the body has a limited life, the soul lives forever. The relationship between the soul and the body is like that of a driver and a car. One cannot do without the other. By itself the soul can do nothing. In the same way, the car cannot move about without the driver. The soul, like any driver, brings with it knowledge and experience of the past lives, and desires to drive the car accordingly. However, the body is endowed with a variety of senses that compel it to be attracted to the environment. This causes a conflict between the soul and the body, each winning and losing depending upon the circumstances. The car wears out with use. Finding it no longer useful the soul leaves it to take on a new body through another birth.

AURA

The word: aura is used to describe the distinctive atmosphere of a place, person or thing. In relation to the human personality the word is used to describe a supposedly invisible force surrounding the person. The word is frequently used in parapsychology and refers to a subtle field of luminous multi-coloured radiation surrounding a person like a halo. It is said to represent or be composed of vibrations emerging from the individual and reflects the person's thoughts and feelings. It is contended that specific meanings can be derived from different colours of the aura. Together they reflect the emotions of the person.

Some people believe that auras could be viewed by the naked eye. However, this is a controversial claim. Most people disagree with it. It is also believed that the auras reflect personality traits and also physical health. This is possible because good health is an essential element of a magnetic personality. It is also explained that auras cannot be seen in total darkness, or if the person or object is not directly visible. Modern metaphysics explains that the aura represents the electromagnetic field. This can be demonstrated through Kirlian photography.

Kirlian photography is named after Semyon Kirlian who discovered that when an object placed on a photographic plate is connected to a source of high voltage, small corona discharges create an image on the plate. Kirlian's work is often referred to as "electrography", "electro-photography" and also "corona discharge photography". According to Kirlian, the images of living objects were proof of the *life force* or aura that surrounds all living beings. He demonstrated his concept through photographs of a fresh leaf, and how the images gradually vanished when the leaf gradually dried. An important aspect of Kirlian photography was the ability to show the acupuncture points in the human body. There are many who do not agree with Kirlian's work and offer alternative explanations. However, his work seriously drew attention to the possibility of a magnetic field around every person.

> **Think it over...**
>
> Every man is valued in this world as he shows by his conduct he wishes to be valued.
>
> — *Bruyère*

MESMERISM

Franz Anton Mesmer claimed the existence of a magnetic fluid or ethereal medium as a therapeutic agent, and called it *'magnétisme animal'*, meaning *animal magnetism*. He wanted to identify the life force residing in the bodies of animals and human beings, as compared to the magnetic force that was identified with *mineral magnetism*, *cosmic magnetism* and *planetary magnetism*. The words animal magnetism was later replaced with mesmerism, though Mesmer never coined or used the word.

Mesmer had opponents, who did not agree with him. A French Royal Commission put his work to test. While it was agreed that the cures he claimed were genuine, the Commission was not convinced with the existence of a magnetic fluid. Could it be the work of imagination? Or that of hypnosis and autosuggestion? It is now agreed that mesmerism and hypnosis are different concepts altogether. The word: mesmerize is often used when a person captures the attention of others completely.

REIKI

Reiki is an alternate therapy for the treatment of physical, emotional and mental diseases. Developed by Mikao Usui in Japan in 1922, practitioners use their hands to pass "healing energy" to bring about healing. The practitioner can heal others and also self.

Reiki is the combination of two Japanese words, 'rei' meaning universal, and 'ki' meaning energy or life force. Reiki is the therapeutic method that uses the energy to heal human beings, animals and plants. It is based upon the existence of a universal energy, or "life force". Everyone can access this energy provided a Reiki Master attunes the person to do so. The attunement is provided in three steps. Once attuned, the practitioner can pass the energy through the palms by placing them at different parts of the body, or even without touching the patient with the palms a few centimeters away from the affected portion. Reiki is a positive form of energy and can also be sent to recipients living far away. Children can also learn to use this energy. Since the energy comes from the universe, it is inexhaustible.

All practitioners are advised to follow five Reiki principles:

1. Always be grateful
2. Work hard
3. Be kind to others
4. Do not get angry
5. Do not worry.

Since Reiki uses universal energy as a healing medium it is described as an energy therapy. Although it is emphasized that it has a scientific basis using electromagnetic forces, it is not without its opponents who are not convinced with its efficacy. They argue that with momentary relief people may overlook serious problems requiring conventional treatment. However, Reiki practitioners agree that patients can use conventional treatment and Reiki simultaneously.

Popularity of Reiki is evident from its widespread use around the world. It confirms the existence of a "life force" and universal energy that can be used in a variety of ways.

CHAKRA

The chakra, meaning a wheel, discus or a circle, refers to a focal point that receives, assimilates and expresses life force energy, and pertains to the centres of activity on the spinal cord of a human being. Popularly described as seven in number, the chakras span from the base of the spine to the top of the head. Chakras are mentioned in the Vedas, the Upanishads and other Hindu religious texts. They direct the biophysical energy in the body. It is said that the chakras need to be energized through yoga. The energy that emanates rises from the lower levels to the higher levels leading one even to enlightenment. Hindus refer to it as the awakening of the Kundalini, which lies dormant until awakened. It rises upward through various chakras leading one to divinity.

While thinkers around the world have acknowledged chakras, or energy focal points, they have been interpreted and used differently around the world. One is led to read about the Tantric model, the Buddhist model and the Chinese models, each with some variations and modifications. Some connect them with the endocrine system that controls vital functions in the body through hormones. What is significant is that various systems acknowledge that there are vital energy points spread in the human body, and that these need to be energized for the person to achieve the full potential. It is also agreed that one gets sick or unwell when the balance between these energy centres is disturbed. Various medical streams direct efforts to re-establish the harmony between these centres of energy and create wellness. This knowledge is important to the person desiring to develop a magnetic personality.

> **Think it over...**
>
> Lives of all great men remind us, we can make our lives sublime.
>
> — *Longfellow*

CHARISMA

Charisma refers to the charm that inspires admiration and enthusiasm in other people. It is a word that describes the salient quality of individuals with a magnetic personality. It is popularly believed that this quality is a gift of nature or a divine favour. Such people possess the ability to charm, inspire, persuade and influence others, making them natural leaders.

Everyone admires these qualities, but politicians, people from show business, top executives, public speakers, coaches and academicians especially desire knowledge about the making of a magnetic personality. Psychologists and sociologists are particularly interested in what makes a person charismatic. This quality has been used for the benefit of mankind, but also for destruction as we see in the case of Adolf Hitler and other dictators.

Studies reveal that charismatic people experience personal emotions strongly. They are enthusiastic and fill others with enthusiasm. They believe in what they do, and are not easily influenced by others.

Contrary to what the majority feel, charisma can be developed just like other qualities. When an actor can act charismatic on stage or on screen, why can't a person develop charisma or a magnetic personality through study and effort? Many qualities contribute to the development of a magnetic personality. We have already seen that there are reservoirs of energy within each individual. Forces of magnetism that attract and repel influence mankind as much as they do the earth and the universe, maintaining a state of equilibrium. The earth itself is a big magnet with north and south poles, which are used to chart one's way around the world.

In the steps that follow we will try to understand the qualities that contribute to the development of a magnetic personality, and how an average person can use these in life to find great happiness and fulfilment.

POINTS TO PONDER

1. To develop personal magnetism one must begin from wherever one is today.
2. Nothing can be achieved without the willingness and effort to change.
3. Unaware of it, everyone simultaneously projects different images.
4. Self-development begins with knowledge of the self. Know your strengths and weaknesses.
5. All objects and beings have magnetic qualities.
6. Positive and negative vibrations emerge from all beings.

7. Magnets are known to influence human reaction and behaviour.
8. Electricity is widely used to analyse and correct human reactions.
9. People with similar temperaments are attracted to each other.
10. The human body is a complex structure controlled by the soul.
11. Every person is believed to have a magnetic field.
12. Reiki practitioners contend that the positive vibrations from the "universal life force" can correct the imbalance in living beings.
13. Ancient Hindu literature describes ways of activating the latent energy within human beings.
14. Charisma can be developed like other human qualities.

Essentials of Personal Magnetism

The desire to look attractive is attributed more to women than to men. In reality, it is a common human desire to be attractive. People will go all out to achieve it. Everyone desires to impress others from the word 'go'. First impressions could often be deceptive. However, the ability to project a good first impression is a bold step that makes it easier to be favourably accepted by others. We need to understand personal magnetism in greater depth.

What is it that makes a person attractive? A person is said to be attractive when one possesses qualities, which delight us both visually or mentally. This gives rise to other questions. What qualities please us most? Are these qualities a gift of nature, or can anyone develop them through personal effort? Are these qualities temporary or can they be made to last a lifetime?

Many people are born beautiful. They have an attractive set of features. Yet experience tells us that these are not enough. A beautiful person draws attention, but may not be able to hold this attention for long. To be truly attractive, one needs to possess many other qualities that draw from resources deep within us. God has made all things beautiful. He has blessed everyone with a reservoir of deep inner beauty that can help make one more attractive. We need to understand the simple rules of life, and follow them to develop a magnetic personality.

GOOD HEALTH

Good health is essential to developing personal magnetism. The human body is a complex structure that depends upon several well-defined functions before it can radiate good health and charm.

The body depends upon the digestive system to provide nourishment to every part. If the food we eat is varied enough to achieve that then there is no need for concern. It does not always happen that way. Social pressures, habits and tastes drift one away from what nature desires. Many of us eat more than what we require. A large number eat what is not good for us. The wrong kind of food could release toxins that make the organs sluggish and rob the body of its buoyancy. The food must provide sufficient roughage to keep the digestive tract clean and functioning well. Milk, fruits and vegetables are rich sources of vital substances that affect the skin, hair, eyes, and the organs. They must form a good part of the daily diet. Emotions have a marked effect upon the digestive system. Therefore, one must be calm during a meal, and until the food is digested.

Some physical exercise must form a part of daily routine. Walking, swimming and various forms of physical work provide good exercise to keep a person trim. Exercise helps increase one's breathing capacity. The deeper one breathes, more oxygen is available for the blood to absorb and pass on to the tissues in the body. A shallow breather cannot look rosy and healthy. You could begin each day with breathing near the window of your bedroom. Gradually your breathing capacity will increase to add on to your personal power.

Along with the need for physical fitness there is the need for emotional well-being. One will do well to understand personal limitations. If one is weak in a particular area, it should not let you feel dejected and run-down. You should learn to live with these limitations. Nature has spared no pains to make the human body perfect. When we burden it with a load that is heavier than what it can bear, stress affects the weaker areas, robbing it of vitality. It is essential to adopt a lifestyle that is in harmony with one's health and ability.

SELF-ESTEEM

How do you rate yourself? Are you content with your appearance, your physique, health, education, and environments? If you do not rate yourself well, you cannot expect others to do so. Unless you believe you are attractive, you cannot be attractive to anyone. To be attractive, you must understand the ways of nature. Nature has made everyone and everything beautiful. If we are not satisfied with what nature has made us, it is our fault. We meddle with it though the demands are few and simple. We must live in harmony with it.

You must accept yourself as you are. God had a purpose in sending you to this world. He had a purpose in making you what you are. How you feel about it depends upon you. You have your choice. You can look up at what you are. You could also feel dejected about what you are. It is all in your attitude. When you are positive, an optimist, you generate positive vibrations that add to your power and make you attractive. If you accept to be negative, a pessimist, who sees little hope, you have company of a lot of people who do not possess a magnetic personality.

SELF-CONFIDENCE

Self-confidence is closely linked with self-esteem. It is another essential element to develop a magnetic personality. Millions of capable persons fail to rise because of lack of self-confidence. They enjoy low self-esteem because of their negative thoughts about their appearance, the family background or because they cannot forget an unpleasant past. To develop a magnetic personality these trivial thoughts must be overcome. Through control of one's thoughts, feelings and actions it is possible to adopt new habits and develop self-confidence.

To develop confidence, evaluate your abilities periodically. Review your achievements and failures. Improve upon your past performances. You need to revise estimates of your personality. Your personality will grow with effort. Devote more time on activities where you have achieved success. Acquire knowledge that can help you achieve still greater success. Try a hand at new activities. Success is the best confidence builder. Keep repeating your successes. Never let doubts cloud your mind and faith in your abilities. Develop new interests. Read books on new subjects. Join a club. Learn to sing, or play a musical instrument. Go out where you can meet new people. Your confidence will grow.

Think it over...

Confidence imparts a wondrous inspiration to its possessor. It bears him on in security, either to meet no danger, or to find matter of glorious trial.

—*Milton*

BODY LANGUAGE

Body gestures convey more than words. People speak with their eyes. Some convey a message through silence and a smile. Others convey their disapproval without speaking a word. You can get to know when people are happy, sad, angry, disheartened, disapproving, or whatever. Facial expressions and the body language tell a lot about a person.

A positive body language is an essential element of personal magnetism. You can read the levels of confidence from the body language of individuals. When negotiating, people gain advantage over others through their ability to read body language. Everyone knows that a good posture and carriage make one attractive, so do good manners and a genial temperament. One is attracted to individuals who smile effortlessly and speak convincingly. People who have their backs hunched, or stand leaning against walls and furniture cannot look attractive. The way a person sits, walks, greets and meets people goes a long way to be attractive to others.

The face is the focal point of attraction. It is also an index of one's thoughts. The power to attract emerges from the thoughts. Controlled thinking influences personal development and success. Just as happiness and gaiety attract goodwill and well-being, feelings of anxiety, worry, anger and envy leave their telltale marks on the face. One must project a happy state of mind to radiate the inner beauty of self.

PERSONAL GROOMING

Personal grooming helps make men, women and children attractive. A bath everyday ensures cleanliness and freedom from body odour. It is not necessary that a person should be obsessed with personal grooming, as some people are, but it is important that a person must have the hair trimmed, oiled and combed, the teeth cleaned, the nails trimmed, and project a general feeling of pleasantness. Men must shave regularly just as the ladies need to manage the hair well, have neat eyebrows and wear light makeup to look attractive. If a man sports a moustache or a beard, it must be trimmed and maintained. It is generally all right to have a manicure once a fortnight and a haircut once a month. Women too need to visit a beauty salon regularly.

DRESS SENSE

The way a person dresses draws immediate attention. Clothes speak loudly of one's dress sense and attitude. Clothes enhance the influence of body language. However, the elegance of dress does not necessarily come from expensive clothes. Clean, crisp clothes worn without much fuss enhances personal charm. Simplicity is always appreciated.

One must dress as well as one can afford to. Clothes convey a person's tastes, disposition, likes and dislikes.

They help to attract immediate attention. Like personal charm, clothes must delight the eye and the mind. One must dress to suit the occasion. Clothes must be comfortable to wear, easy to care for, and elegant to look at. Expensive fabrics need not always be attractive, but most are easy to care for and last better. Clothes of good quality permit maximum wearing. Clothes that fit well and are well cared for always attract second glances. One should not wear the same clothes day after day. They must be alternated to get uniform wear.

Think it over...

Man must build his culture about the complete human personality....Whatever nourishes the personality, humanizes it, refines it, deepens it, intensifies its aptitude and broadens its field of action is good; whatever limits it or thwarts it, whatever sends it back into tribal patterns and limits its capacity for human cooperation and communion must be counted as bad.

— *Lewis Mumford*

EDUCATION

Everyone would immediately acknowledge that a person who desires to develop personal magnetism must be educated. But what does being educated mean? To most people going through school and perhaps attaining a degree in a college means that one is educated. There are millions of people who have not opened a book after leaving school or college. It is true that they may be gainfully employed. They may be making a livelihood through whatever they learnt earlier. Yet their knowledge is restricted to whatever knowledge they have put to use, and forgotten part of what they might have learnt at school and college.

The word: education is derived from the Latin word *educare*, which means 'to rear'. Education is the process of preparing a person to use personal capabilities buried deep within each one. Certificates, diplomas and degrees are no more than a document stating the level of study a person has undergone. What is more important is how much of the knowledge so gained has been utilised by the person to attain what he or she wants to. Whatever has been learnt at school and college should form the foundation of true education. Through it one should bring forth from within ideas that benefit the person, and also mankind. Such education helps one to use one's imagination and creativity. The right type of education would help develop a magnetic personality.

VISION

To develop personal magnetism one needs to look ahead. It is not sufficient to think in terms of one's everyday routine, or even looking at a month or a few months ahead. One needs to have a focussed vision where a person has definite long-term goals, which are sub-divided into short-term goals, annual goals, quarterly goals, monthly goals and weekly goals.

To have vision is to be able to think about and look at the future with imagination and wisdom. A successful person looks at life with a much wider perspective than most people. Besides looking ahead the person looks to every aspect of life. While there are personal goals to fulfil personal needs, the person with a vision also sets family goals, career goals, community goals and retirement goals.

Goals are the key to success. When goals are adopted and written down they set into motion a success mechanism that takes one towards greater achievement. All successful individuals, groups and companies work by setting goals at every level of operations. When the vision is based upon experience and farsightedness, the success one attains is significantly outstanding.

COMMUNICATION SKILLS

A person may be knowledgeable, experienced and wise, but if one is unable to communicate effectively with others, one can attain nothing. Effective communication is an essential element to develop personal magnetism.

Communication is the act or process of communicating, the imparting or exchanging of thoughts, opinions or information. It also refers to something imparted, interchanged or transmitted. Generally, it refers to the use of speech or writing, as is done through verbal or written messages from person to person, as on telephone, or through facsimile machine or post.

Besides communicating verbally people also communicate feelings and emotions to others. This need not be through vocal or written messages, but by their sheer presence. Human emotions are equally responsive to communication, being sensitive to both the positive and negative forms. Sharing of intimate thoughts and feelings influences human beings.

Communication cannot be restricted only to the spoken or written word. Much is communicated through silence, when one uses it as a tool to introspect, or talk to oneself. Silence is also used to punish another person by not talking to him or her. This is a common phenomenon amongst couples, or children and parents. Even friends go into the silent mode occasionally to settle personal scores.

People communicate through their actions, clothes and even makeup? Women spend much time in dressing and makeup to appear beautiful. Some wear flowers in their hair. It is common for both men and women to wear fragrances that also convey a message. Just as distant voices come through space and reach us through the radio, people communicate positive and negative vibrations all the time. Even in a temple, a mosque, a church or any other place of prayer people not only pray or pay obeisance to a deity, but experience the great pleasure and peace of receiving positive vibrations from others.

Think it over...

Discretion of speech is more than eloquence; and to speak agreeably to him with whom we deal is more than to speak in good words, or in good order.

— *Bacon*

SPEAKING SKILLS

Although speaking skills are a part of communication skills in general, these are especially mentioned because of their importance in helping develop personal magnetism. The earliest book on public speaking was written more than 2000 years ago. Speaking skills formed a part of the teaching curriculum at that time. Although not taught specifically as a subject in schools and colleges, public speaking is important in everyday life. Many make up for lack of learning by taking classes in later life.

Speaking skills are closely linked with leadership skills. People look forward to hear leaders even when they are not orators. Mahatma Gandhi, Mother Teresa and several others possessed leadership qualities. As leaders they stood high above others. They had risen above personal needs, made outstanding sacrifices and above all else thought from the point of view of the common man. People looked forward to hear them.

Leaders lead by example, not only by speech. A leader benefits through good speaking skills. On the other hand, a speaker is more effective when he or she possesses leadership qualities. Speaking skills and leadership qualities are closely linked. To make the audience act on a proposed idea, the audience must be convinced that the speaker has put into practice what he wants them to do. The audience is always willing to follow an accepted leader. Even if the speaker is new to the audience but his credentials highlight leadership characteristics, the audience will find it easier to accept him and the suggestions.

An aspiring speaker is never content to learn only the basics of public speaking. To be effective the speaker will need to develop personal magnetism to become a model person who can inspire and motivate others by the example of personal life. Just as the personality develops, one can use speaking skills with greater authority.

ETIQUETTE AND MANNERS

One cannot imagine a person devoid of etiquette and good manners to have a magnetic personality. Etiquette refers to conventional requirements as to social behaviour. It aims at dignity for everyone. It exemplifies good breeding, acceptance of morals and good taste. Manners indicate the way one acts. They reflect the style and habits of a person. They pertain to the person's outward behaviour.

While a country lives in discipline on the basis of its constitution and the laws enacted to implement it, the society lives in harmony on the basis of the etiquette and manners that have developed through experience, customs and traditions.

People deal with each other at all levels in the society. Since they can sometimes be selfish and can cause unnecessary offence by hurting the feelings of others, mankind has evolved these unwritten guidelines to maintain harmony in relationships amongst people. These guidelines are developed on the concept of being thoughtful towards everyone. They are guided by the thoughtful question, "Is it fair to all concerned?"

Etiquette and manners may not mean much to many. They are like a lubricant. Just as a drop of oil stops a moving part from screeching, they help in smoothening relationships between people. A person with a magnetic personality cannot do without them.

HUMILITY

Another element that contributes to personal magnetism is humility. One is always attracted to a humble person. Irrespective of how high a position one may hold, or the great fortunes and wealth that one may possess and control, one is attracted by humility.

Some of the greatest people of all time were not acknowledged because of their knowledge, wealth or position, but because of their humility. Mahatma Gandhi, Mother Teresa, Swami Vivekanand, Nelson Mandela, Abraham Lincoln and many more were recognised for their humility, for their feelings towards mankind.

Humility is the quality of being humble. To be humble means to be modest or to have a low estimate of one's personal importance. However, to be humble should not be mistaken to have low self-esteem. While self-esteem refers to one's personal estimate of the self, humility pertains to the comparison between the self and others. Humility keeps in check one's pride that tends to inflate into arrogance over a period. A humble person rises above the feeling of 'self'. One takes credit for achievements not as a doer, but only as a medium to make them possible.

Saint Augustine rightly proclaimed, "It was pride that changed angels to devils; it is humility that makes men as angels."

Think it over...

The body of our prayer is the sum of our duty; and as we must ask of God whatsoever we need, so we must watch and labour for all that we ask.

— *Jeremy Taylor*

THE LOVE OF GOD

When a person is humble, one bows in love before God. A person with a magnetic personality draws great strength from the association with God, a powerful force, which controls the whole universe. One cannot understand, comprehend or describe this force completely. All religions acknowledge that we can draw great personal strength from Him. The greatest of men and women of all times have done that. People believe that God was within these great men and women, to guide and provide them with strength. This makes one wonder if everyone can draw on His strength to develop greater personal power. The religions advocate that to draw on His strength, one must follow the path of truthfulness, honesty, and thoughtfulness of others.

God is to be found everywhere. He is a part of this vast natural world. The closer we are to nature, the more we can draw upon Him. We derive strength by developing an aesthetic sense for beautiful things handed down to us by nature. The beauty of the snow-clad peaks, the greenery of a thick forest, the shiny surface of a quiet lake, or the multi-coloured grandeur of a well laid out garden soothe us physically and emotionally, giving us great strength. This explains why people move away from cities to holiday resorts to be closer to nature. The more one can draw from it, the better it is.

The person who needs to develop personal magnetism cannot afford to ignore this unending source of power. One must spend a few moments every day in quiet conversation with God. People talk to Him as one would to a friend. They seek solutions to their problems. They seek His peace and blessings. The response may not come immediately, but it will come. When in distress, comfort yourself with the thought that with God on your side you have the most powerful force with you. There is nothing to fear. God will help cross the hurdles of life.

BEING RESPONSIBLE

A characteristic of people who develop a magnetic personality is their high sense of responsibility towards other people and situations. This is a rare quality. These people are reliable in that they will fulfil whatever responsibility they undertake. These people are mature in the sense that they will take responsibility when things go wrong. They do not hesitate to say "sorry". One would think that maturity and the sense of personal responsibility would only come with age, and therefore these qualities would show up in later life. It is not so. It has been observed even in school-going children. When parents inculcate the habit of acting responsible with people and situations to their children, they are really helping them to develop personal appreciation and magnetism. One is immediately attracted to these children. In due course they become responsible citizens with great personal magnetism.

PERSONAL RELATIONSHIPS

It is interesting to note that while individuals eager to develop personal magnetism are doing so to attract the attention and the goodwill of people, much of the force they enjoy comes from their existing personal relationships. This means that as they develop more relationships their personal magnetism grows simultaneously.

There are three distinct areas of life where people develop relationships. The first one pertains to the family. It can undoubtedly be said that the family is the primary institution on which the foundation of civilization stands. Around the world, there are marked differences in family life from one area to another, and from one culture to another. In many developed countries the price that people have had to pay for economic freedom and prosperity is the breakdown of the family. In many countries special emphasis is being given to strengthen family ties. Within the nuclear family there is the husband, wife and children. However, in cultures where joint families are prevalent there are parents, in-laws, uncles, aunts and cousins. Within these families each member contributes to the strength of others, and vice versa.

The second area of relationships is at the workplace. The sizes of the offices vary and so do the number of employees or colleagues. Some offices are small and there is a close-knit relationship between the workers. However, many are employed with the larger companies that have many employees. In general, one needs to work and develop relationships with colleagues who work at the same level, those that are subordinate and those who are at a senior position. Great effort is required to acquire the skills necessary to handle different kinds of relationships at the workplace. Those who do well rise in position quickly. A marked change in the workplace over the years is that there is greater emphasis on teamwork rather than individual activity. Developing relationships within the teams has become important to ensure higher productivity and success.

The third area of personal relationship is the society. People are members in housing societies, clubs, trade organizations, social welfare associations, educational institutions and others. Besides these, everyone needs to build relationships with different kinds of service providers, grocery and provision stores, and people like the guards who protect buildings, the liftmen, the gardeners and domestic help. The people come from different backgrounds, have different levels of education and require a variety of ways to build good relationships with them. Sometimes it is a challenge. But that is what life is all about. Good relationship means better personal development.

Think it over...

The improvement of our way of life is more important than the spreading of it. If we make it satisfactory enough, it will spread automatically. If we do not, no strength of arms can permanently impose it.

— *Charles A. Lindbergh*

DESIRE FOR SELF-IMPROVEMENT

The person with a magnetic personality knows that there is no end to learning and self-improvement in life. When young people leave school to go to college they get their first experience of freedom from the rigid discipline of the school. The education in colleges is focussed on lesser subjects than in school, and this sends out a wrong signal that we do not need to remember everything we learnt at school. This is not true. Whatever is taught in school provides the foundation of education for life. The study at college prepares one for a career. That too is never enough. One needs to update knowledge regularly.

Have you ever noticed that doctors and professionals attend seminars to update their knowledge periodically? Have you seen the books lined in the offices of legal practitioners? Many more are added every year. Without them the practitioner would soon be outdated. Even in the field of business people update their knowledge through trade magazines and periodicals. The larger business houses have their own training departments where the managers are provided information on the latest developments in the field. Even the small companies are taking advantage of training facilities provided by specialised consultancy companies that provide such services.

To maintain personal magnetism it is not sufficient to be curious and inquisitive. It is necessary to be eager to acquire new knowledge. To be able to do this people need to read regularly. The reading is not restricted to one's field of specialisation alone but extends to every aspect of life. People subscribe to magazines and buy books of interest. A person who wants to go ahead must read at least one book every month. Half of these could pertain to one's field of work and to self-improvement. The rest could be reading for pleasure.

A BALANCED LIFE

Another essential element to develop personal magnetism is a balanced life. There are four distinct fields of interest in a person's life. To be well appreciated the person must devote ample attention to each of these activities. In the absence of balance the life becomes lopsided and the balance tilts in one direction.

The first field of attention is one's own life. It is necessary that a person must devote sometime everyday to personal needs and care. A part of this time must be devoted to personal development and growth. Unfortunately, most people either devote too much time or ignore personal life altogether. Everyone will agree that either of the choices is wrong.

The second field of attention is the time and activities with the family. We cannot overlook that the purpose of work and life is to raise a good family. It is here that the future citizens of a country are learning to run the world. All the good things, and also the bad, that we see in the society today are the result of what these persons were taught in their homes years ago. Keeping this in view, one must devote ample time to the home.

Bringing up a family is the joint responsibility of the husband and wife. Neither can shun responsibility. Men and women are built differently. They possess different skills. They need to work as a team, and not as individuals. When the children grow up they too become a part of the team and learn to share united responsibility for the home. This way they become responsible citizens. Unfortunately, it is to be observed that most men do not devote sufficient time and attention to the family. Even workingwomen are guilty of not giving quality time to the family. Is it fair to all concerned?

The third field of attention is the time and activities at the workplace. A person's vocation is the source of the family's livelihood. The harder a person works the greater are the rewards. Therefore, there is every reason for individuals to devote greater time and effort at the workplace than in other fields of activity. Besides earning money, a person is able to achieve a special kind of satisfaction at the workplace when one is able to use one's creativity and imagination to produce outstanding achievements. The deep sense of achievement tends to attract individuals to become workaholics. This is true of both men and women. Herein lies the danger of the person losing the sense of balance and devoting greater attention to one's vocation. One forgets the purpose of work. One forgets that money has its own limitations. Some things cannot be bought with money. Many realise it late that money is a good slave, but a poor master.

The fourth field of attention is the time and activities in the society where we live. No one can live a secluded life without contact with others. At every point a person needs to interact with people – the domestic help, the liftman, the guard, the gardener and others. People need to deal with bus conductors, taxi drivers, the sale staff in the stores and elsewhere. There is the need to know and deal with people in housing societies, clubs and institutions. Some do it well. There are others who just make do. Unfortunately, some begin to find greater pleasure in these activities. Have you observed how some people become self-appointed social reformers and society managers, and devote much more time than is necessary on these activities than on other fields of activities. People inclined towards politics and social services are particularly guilty of this. With greater time spent in this field the balance of life is likely to become lopsided.

The secret of developing a balanced personality depends upon creating a fair balance between the four activities that pre-occupy the lives of almost everyone.

POINTS TO PONDER

1. Good health is a primary need to develop a magnetic personality.
2. If you do not rate yourself well, do not expect others to do so.
3. Self-confidence is the foundation of a magnetic personality.
4. Body language speaks louder than words.
5. Dress and personal grooming attract immediate attention.
6. Education should prepare a person to use the latent abilities.
7. One must look at the future with imagination and wisdom.
8. There can be no success without effective communication.
9. A skillful speaker is able to persuade others.
10. Etiquette and good manners help smoothen relationships with everyone.
11. Humility and the love of God are unending sources of power.
12. The ability to handle responsibility leads a person to continued success.
13. Good personal relationships promote personal magnetism.
14. Self-improvement should be a lifetime process.
15. A balanced life is an ideal life.

Physical Health

A magnetic personality emerges from a combination of several distinct characteristics that have been identified and can be developed to enhance one's personality. It is not enough only to know what contributes to develop the personality. One must know how to do it. Along with a deeper understanding of each factor that contributes to the development of the personality, one will need the determination to change the circumstances that might be holding one back. To accept and bring about change one needs personal discipline. Nothing can be achieved without it.

Both physical and emotional health contributes towards personal magnetism. Is anything possible without good health? Johnson explained it simply, "To preserve health is a moral and religious duty, for health is the basis of all social virtues. We can no longer be useful when not well."

Unfortunately, with competition to get ahead, most people place a much greater burden on the body than what it can really bear. Endowed with great resilience, the body makes every effort to cope with the burden placed upon it, but it is not long before the 'safety valve' blows, and one begins to experience ill health and disease. Many like to describe the situation as 'dis-ease', a situation created by personal carelessness. Others describe the situation as 'burn out'.

HABITS – GOOD AND BAD

Every person is a product of the cumulative effect of one's habits, both good and bad. People are known and judged by their habits. Good and bad habits together project a mixed image of an individual. While good habits contribute towards enhancing the personality, bad habits detract from it. The immediate concern of person who desires a magnetic personality is as simple as to develop additional good habits, and to eliminate bad ones.

A habit is an act a person is accustomed to. Through sheer repetition a person's actions become a habit, a part of everyday life. The act must have been just a thought. The thought conjured an image, a dream. This dream created a desire that in turn motivated the person to act. Both good and bad habits have a similar beginning. For example, the suffering of a person may arouse a thought of compassion, and this may motivate an individual to help the person. The act of helping a needy person would be satisfying. When repeated, the individual would develop the habit of being compassionate. In the same way, when a young person thinks of trying an alcoholic drink for the first time, one does not realise that if not controlled, this could be the beginning to the bad habit of drinking, or even alcoholism.

The human body follows a definite system to adopt a habit. When a young person decides to learn cycling it seems an impossible task. How could one balance on two wheels? However, encouraged by watching others enjoying the thrill of cycling, one ventures to try it out. In the beginning one does not know whether to concentrate on the handle bar and watch where the cycle is going, or look at the pedals that need to be kept moving to keep the bicycle in motion. There is also the brake that needs attention to stop the cycle in an emergency. The initial efforts are conscious efforts. Since one can concentrate only on one thing at a time, there is confusion. However, when one repeats the actions to keep the cycle going, the subconscious takes over, coordinating each action like moving the pedals, controlling the handle bar and also balancing the cycle. The subconscious can handle several things at one time. Through repetition one becomes so adept at cycling that one can do it effortlessly, enjoying the thrill of motion and speed. At this point one can say that cycling has become a habit. One may not ride a cycle for ten years, and yet when one does it again, the subconscious automatically takes over, and one is able to cycle comfortably.

Other habits are no different. Without being aware of it, over a period, one develops a variety of habits pertaining to one's food, clothing, rest, sleep, health, work, personal relationships and a whole lot of other things. Together these influence the life and image of a person. To take control over one's habits one needs to understand how they are affecting the person. One needs to go through a self-analysis to identify personal strengths and weaknesses.

To develop a new habit one needs to perform a particular act repeatedly. It may appear to be an unpleasant thing to do initially. For example, when a person decides to develop a healthy, muscular body it may be necessary to join a gym. The exercises may appear rather tedious to begin with, but one soon gets used to them, and gradually increases the frequency. Besides the exercise it may also be necessary to supplement the normal food with high protein supplements to develop muscle mass. One may not like the taste of the food supplements in the beginning. The desire for a muscular body becomes a source of motivation, and one soon develops the habit of taking the food supplement without fuss.

To get rid of a bad habit one needs to avoid doing it. This is not easy because the subconscious mind will goad one to do it. Under such circumstances one will have to repeatedly make a conscious effort to avoid the act until such time as the subconscious can be retuned. One needs to visualize the harm the bad habit can do. The conscious mind then prevents the act being performed. Through repeated effort one is able to break the habit. You could follow these simple steps to break a bad habit:

- Identify the bad habit. Remind yourself of the harm it is doing you.
- Admit that you have a bad habit. Resolve that you will break it.
- Tell people what you have resolved to do. When you go wrong, people will remind you about it.
- Try to identify the causes for the bad habit. How did it get started? Who could have encouraged you to it? What makes you behave as you do?
- Accept the fact that all bad habits can be broken through effort and perseverance.
- Think of the benefits that will accrue when you break the habit.

- Your efforts to break the habit must be at one go. You can't say, "I will not chew tobacco. Instead I will smoke a mild cigarette." This way you break one habit, and develop another. Break it at one go.
- Talk about the bad habit. Ask people who indulge in it to break it. They may or may not listen to your advice. However, talking about it will affirm your own decision to break it.
- Whenever you feel weak and are tempted to indulge yourself, seek the help of God. He is looking at you all the time.

Think it over...

The chains of habit are generally too small to be felt until they are too strong to be broken.

— *Johnson*

TAKE CONTROL

Before a person can take a firm step towards changing the personality by developing good habits and eliminating bad ones, it is necessary that the person take complete control. One single factor that holds back most people from attaining success is their bad habit of blaming other people and situations for their failure. These people blame everyone and everything for success having eluded them. They will never admit that they are responsible for their failure.

Just take a look at your activities today. Are they not aimed at making things better for you tomorrow, and the day after? Are we not working for a better future? We are doing it today, and we will do it again tomorrow. In the same way, we worked yesterday, the day before and even years earlier. We are today what we worked for yesterday. If we are not content with what we are, let us not look for reasons in others, but within ourselves. Irrespective of age, a truly mature person accepts responsibility for whatever one is today. One should not hesitate to accept that one could have been wrong. One should be willing to make amends. One should be ready for change. One should be ready to get ahead in life.

BE YOURSELF

A common problem with the majority is that people are not what they want to be. They are many people in one. People see and accept them in different forms. The situation becomes worse because people are not in harmony with the self. The cause is easy to understand. Everyone is trying to condition the other in harmony with one's thoughts and perception. The parents, the teachers, friends and others are busy trying to condition each other all the time. You could be as guilty of doing the same to others. One forgets that every person is unique. There never was one like you earlier, there isn't one like you today, nor there ever will be one in the future. Nature has made everyone unique. It is believed that everyone is at a different level of evolution. How could anyone be like the others?

The process of conditioning indulged in by the vast majority leads people to unnecessarily make comparisons amongst each other. This only creates confusion and mental restlessness. It makes people feel inferior. To avoid unpleasant situation people try to conform to others. The price one pays for this peace is suppressed feelings and personal displeasure. One finds only temporary happiness by conforming to others. The suppressed feelings lead to building up of pressure within a person like a volcano ready to erupt.

Take control and be yourself. You are unique. Accept this fact and do not try to be what you are not. Do not let anyone force you into anything. This is your life. Live, as you would like to. Do it your way. Become the magnetic person you eagerly look forward to be. Let nothing hold you back. You are the master of your own life.

THE HUMAN BODY

The human body is a piece of perfection. God has spared no pains to make it that way. Provided that it receives the necessary nutrition and care it is self-sustaining. It can withstand a lot of abuse. Through its in-built immune system it can protect itself against disease and sickness. If there is a major failure, it can cope up with that also. For example, if one of the kidneys fails, the other becomes larger and takes over the work of both the kidneys. If a part of the liver is damaged, the rest of it continues to look after the body needs. When greater stress is placed upon the heart, it still copes with it by increasing its size. In the event of loss of eyesight the body copes by making other senses like those of hearing, smell and touch sharper. When a person loses a hand one learns to work with the other. Even when a person loses both hands, people are known to cope by using their feet to do precise activities like drawing, painting and also playing musical instruments. What more can a person expect from this human body?

Rather than accept the many abilities of the human body as a blessing and live a life of gratitude, most people take them for granted. They burden the body with activities that it cannot bear. Should we be surprised if it gets stressed and begins to fail? Why do we turn a blind eye towards the warning signs it sends us by way of fatigue and little 'aches and pains'? Why do we not make amends in time? Must we take heed only when we reach a point of no return? Most people do not need to be questioned. They are already aware of these questions, and many more. Unfortunately, they are too busy and pre-occupied to think about them. Providing an answer is of course not possible.

Think it over...

If thou wouldst preserve a sound body, use fasting and walking; if a healthful soul, fasting and praying. Walking exercises the body; praying exercises the soul; fasting cleanses both.

— *Francis Quarles*

HEALTH CONSCIOUSNESS

When people ignore personal health, they are really ignoring 'life'. They may not agree, but they have in reality accepted to gradually commit suicide. They have closed their eyes to the consequences that await them. This is their decision. They may blame other people and the circumstances for the situation they are in, but the truth is that they alone are to blame. It is their life. They have to decide how they want to live it.

People who live a healthy life are conscious of the need for good health. They are conscious of the needs of the human body. They ensure that these are provided. Every person being unique, they are aware of their own strengths and weaknesses. They constantly strive to eliminate the weaknesses in life.

Health consciousness is a habit that develops like any other habit. It begins in the mind as a thought, and transforms into action. Repeated actions turn it into a habit. Some develop health consciousness when still young. Others learn it much later after a setback in health. Nature spares no one.

There can be no health consciousness without a deliberate effort. It may become a habit and one may be known to adhere to it strictly. Yet this habit can be maintained only through determination and personal discipline. This habit is constantly in confrontation with the temptations offered by the senses that rule the human body. The temptations come in many forms and ways. They come too often. They come very persuasively, making it difficult to resist them. It is therefore necessary to be careful about developing health consciousness.

PROTECTING THE BODY

An essential part of health consciousness is to realise the need to protect the human body from damage. Children and the elderly are especially prone to accidents. Visit any hospital, and you will find cases of burns, injuries and fractured bones. Many of these could have been avoided.

Even amongst the young adults the incidence of accidents is on the increase because of unsafe driving habits on the road. Hospitals are full of road accident patients. It was always said that accidents are acts of God and cannot be prevented. It is not true. A large number of accidents can be avoided. They are the result of carelessness. Youngsters love speed. While speed thrills, it also kills. Most young people are not responsible enough to be on the road. Alcohol and drugs affect judgment and response, and are responsible for innumerable accidents. Driving after consuming alcohol or drugs must be avoided.

Lack of sleep and fatigue are also responsible for a lot of accidents everyday. Within the home, leaving children unattended, wrong placement of furniture, reaching out for objects placed high or in difficult positions, or unsafe conditions in the bathroom and kitchen are frequently the cause for accidents. When conditions in the home are conducive to accidents, how can one be safe? The situation deserves special attention.

NUTRITIONAL REQUIREMENTS

From the time a child is born until the time a person dies the body's nutritional requirements will have to be met. Good health is dependent upon proper nutrition.

Food habits vary from one region to another, and amongst different cultures and races. Weather conditions also affect food requirements and habits. One would think that one of the easiest things to provide for a magnetic personality is food. However, it is not true. More people are guilty of bad food habits than for any other cause. Parents indulge children not realising that they are encouraging bad eating habits that will be hard to break in later life. While people tend to over-eat in developed nations and become obese, the people in under-developed countries suffer from malnutrition. It is not that it is difficult to provide correct nutritional requirements, but people eat the wrong kinds of food. The eating times are erratic. People are not health conscious.

Each year millions of dollars are spent on antacids and enzyme tablets to digest the excess food people eat. Besides, a lot of unnecessary chemicals from pesticides and preservatives are consumed along with food. To make the situation worse, people consume large quantities of vitamins, pep-up pills, and anti-anxiety and sleeping tablets. Those obsessed with nutrition consume food supplements. Smoking, chewing tobacco and drugs further aggravate the situation. Is the human body capable of coping up with such chemical intake? The answer is 'no'. It is difficult to estimate the loss this chemical intake causes millions of people around the world. Many diseases are related to the consumption of chemicals.

School children are taught early in life that the human body requires carbohydrates, proteins, some fat, vitamins and minerals. They are also taught that these requirements can easily be obtained from the normal food like cereals, vegetables and fruits, pulses, nuts and milk products. Some prefer to eat eggs, poultry, meat, fish and seafood. Whether it is better to eat a completely vegetarian diet or to include poultry, meat and fish is a debatable issue. One must answer this question for oneself. Choose a diet that pleases you.

Here are a few important observations pertaining to nutrition:

- One must eat a balanced diet that contains whole cereals, fresh fruits and vegetables, nuts and milk or milk products.
- Coarse foods are better than refined foods.
- Fresh food is better than preserved food.
- Junk food is known by that name because they are 'junk'.
- Smaller meals eaten frequently are better than heavy meals taken after long intervals.
- A good breakfast, a light lunch and fair dinner are good for health.
- It is better to eat less rather than overeat.

Just as important as food and nutrition is the intake of water. One must drink sufficient quantity of water during the day.

Think it over...

He, who has health, has hope; and he who has hope has everything.

— *Arabian Proverb*

FRESH AIR AND EXERCISE

Just as correct kind of food is necessary for the human body, there is also the need for fresh air and exercise. Breathing is equated with life. When a person faints, the first thing that one checks is breathing and the pulse. Insufficient breathing is supplemented with oxygen.

To develop personal magnetism one must breathe deeply. Most people are shallow breathers. With lower levels of oxygen there is reduction in vigour and energy. With the air in the larger cities polluted, with low level of oxygen and higher level of pollutants, it is common to see people suffering from respiratory ailments. Breathing exercises help improve the oxygen intake of the body.

Hindu religious texts recommend *pranayam* to develop healthy breathing habits. The word *pranayam* is made of two words, *pran* and *ayama.* The word *pran* means vital air or vital breath. The word *ayama* means to regulate or control. *Pranayam* means regulated or controlled breathing. When one practises *pranayam,* the breathing process is controlled. One inhales deep into the lungs, holds the breath and then gradually exhales. One could also inhale through one nostril, hold the breath and then exhale through the other nostril. This way the lung capacity increases gradually. With increased intake of oxygen one feels more energetic and healthy. The generation of energy promotes confidence and capacity to work.

Exercise is equally important because it ensures the circulation of blood throughout the body, helping renew body cells and tissue. The texture of the muscles improves and one develops a greater capacity to work. The younger people prefer to go to a gym. For good health it is sufficient to walk, swim and cycle. Climbing stairs also provides good exercise. Many vocations involve physical work. Women too get an opportunity to exercise through their household work. It is important to be conscious of the need for exercise. Those involved in sedentary type of work could stretch themselves briefly several times everyday. This helps blood circulation.

CLEANSING THE BODY

To keep fit, cleansing the body of waste matter is just as important as nutrition and exercise. One inhales oxygen from fresh air one breathes, and exhales carbon dioxide. Crowded places like cinema halls where the ventilation is limited to exhaust fans only, have a higher level of carbon dioxide, and can induce breathing problems. Such places must be avoided. Within the home the kitchen and bathrooms need good ventilation.

After the food is digested the waste matter is passed out as faeces through bowel movements. Constipation, a condition when a person experiences difficulty in emptying the bowels, is a common problem that bothers a majority of people. Women suffer more than men. Elderly people with sedentary lifestyle are also prone to this problem. Many people habitually consume laxatives to treat constipation. Just like digestive and pep-up pills millions of dollars are spent each year on laxative pills. The solution does not lie in medication but in correct eating habits. The food must contain sufficient roughage. This can be obtained from eating whole cereals, fresh fruits and vegetables. More than physical distress, people suffer mentally because of a missed bowel movement. The problem should be a matter of concern, and not worry. It can be regulated through adoption of correct eating habits. Follow these simple guidelines:

- Eat a balanced diet that contains enough fibre-rich foods like whole grains, cereals, fresh fruits and vegetables.
- Eat at regular periods to maintain a normal flow in the intestines. Avoid missing a meal. The gap will interrupt the bowel movements.

- Avoid excessive eating of refined and fried foods.
- Eat slowly enjoying the meal. Be relaxed at meal-time.
- Drink plenty of fluids. The fibre in the food absorbs water and aids in bowel movement.
- Avoid excessive coffee, smoking and drinking.
- Do not get addicted to laxatives. Change your food habits instead.

Within the human body kidneys clean the blood by removing the waste matter, which is finally flushed away as urine. Water plays a crucial role in this function. One must have a high intake of fluids, particularly good clean water.

The skin also provides a medium for excretion. It reflects the condition of inner health. It looks sallow or attractive. Its condition changes with age. Sebum, a fatty substance secreted by the cells on the skin surface, helps to keep the skin moist, elastic and healthy. The production of sebum may increase during adolescence, clogging the skin pores. With advancing age, the production reduces, and the skin becomes dry, less elastic, and begins to wrinkle. The skin is the index of inner health and the principal medium that makes a person look attractive. It deserves special protection and care.

The primary need is to keep it clean. One sweats more profusely in the hot summer months. However, dust settles on it and clogs the pores irrespective of the weather. There is nothing better than a bath with plain soap and water to keep it clean and healthy. The process of soaping, rubbing and rinsing with cold or warm water is stimulating. It promotes better circulation of blood in the body.

Massaging the body with oil before a bath helps promote better circulation of blood. It keeps the skin soft and supple. Vigorous massage should be avoided. It may not be possible to massage before each bath, but done occasionally it is useful. For those who perspire profusely, particularly under the arms, an antiperspirant is useful. To ensure freedom from body odours typical in hot and humid weather, a deodorant provides the obvious answer.

Think it over...

Certainly work is not always required of a man. There is such a thing as a sacred idleness – the cultivation of which is now fearfully neglected.

— *G. Macdonald*

RELAXATION AND FATIGUE

The muscular system in the body is responsible for the physical activity by the human body. To make movements and do a variety of jobs, the muscles contract and relax according to need. The longer one works, the more the muscles contract and relax. This causes wear and tear of the muscle cells and also sends signals to the adjacent nerves. This causes fatigue. To overcome fatigue people adopt a variety of ways. They may take a brief rest, drink water, or a cup of tea or coffee. Some use massage to relieve the muscles. At the extreme end there are people who resort to alcohol and drugs. One can observe this with drivers who drive long distances regularly.

To maintain personal efficiency one must learn to find relief from fatigue through relaxation. Relief through use of alcohol and drugs is wrong. These do not relieve one from fatigue. They only make a person insensitive to fatigue and alter one's perception that may lead to lack of judgment of space, distance and time, making one prone to accidents.

A positive attitude and understanding helps one to appreciate how fatigue builds up. For example, it is more restful to walk than stand. Walking allows each leg to rest intermittently. Rather than stand, it is more restful to sit. It is still more comfortable to lie down. Relaxation aims at helping the muscle contraction to loosen up completely. When this is achieved, the adjacent nerves too get to rest. With no nervous activity, relief follows.

Each activity involves different muscles. Only those muscles that are used are prone to fatigue. It is advisable to learn how to relax these muscles lying down in the privacy of one's room. When a person becomes conscious of physical fatigue, one learns to find and use comfortable furniture, adopt a comfortable posture, and also take short periods of rest to avoid fatigue to set in. Physical relaxation promotes mental relation also.

Physical fatigue is easy to recognize because it follows physical activity. It can soon be relieved through rest and sleep. However, fatigue that is caused by emotional stress is different. It is induced by the emotions and is controlled by the mind. Without the least physical exertion, emotional fatigue can set in, making a person feel tired, moody and irritable. This fatigue emerges from monotony and depression. Once it sets in, it becomes difficult to control unless one can take control of the mind.

A short-term remedy lies in drugs recommended by a doctor. The long-term treatment is through control of negative thoughts and habits. This requires effort, but can be achieved. To avoid fatigue one must organise an interesting daily routine and do things that are satisfying. One must develop a friendly attitude towards everyone. When one is happy and balances work and relaxation fatigue vanishes.

SLEEP

Sleep is necessary for good health. Everyone knows this. However, with greater pressures on time, particularly in the larger cities, people are cutting out on sleep. It may appear harmless and easy to cope with initially, but in due course it emerges as a major problem affecting a large number of people.

Lack of sleep is a major cause for many physical and emotional ailments compelling doctors to use drugs that can be addictive and habit-forming. Just like the widespread use of antacids, pep-up pills and laxatives, huge amounts of money are spent annually on sleep inducing medicines. Surprisingly, equally large sums are spent on de-addiction treatment.

Sleep is just as important for the human body as nutrition, exercise or keeping it clean. Sleep helps prepare the human body for yet another day by recharging the battery of physical and emotional well-being. Lack of sleep can drive a person crazy, affecting both physical and emotional health. Very often people want to sleep but are unable to do so. Anxiety and excitement can disturb sleep. Even when they get to sleep, the quality of sleep may not be sufficiently refreshing. One wakes up tired with no enthusiasm to work or do anything.

Relaxation and sleep must be given the importance they deserve. Though sleeping patterns vary, on an average one needs 7 to 8 hours of sleep. Elderly people sleep less, but make up through short naps in the day. Short naps during the day are not practical for most working people. These can be refreshing and can help make up for the lack of sleep at night. The problem of sleeplessness emerges from one's thoughts. If one does not want it to become a problem, it is necessary that the thinking pattern must be changed. One must not cut out on sleep for any reason whatsoever.

If you cannot sleep do not rush to swallow a sleeping pill. Lie on your back making yourself as comfortable as you can. Keep the legs straight. Also stretch out the arms straight with palms downwards. Close your eyes. Start counting from 100 backwards – 100, 99, 98 and so on. Concentrate on the counting. Soon you will fall asleep.

FAMILY DOCTOR

Your family doctor is your best friend for problems relating to health. One must develop a positive relationship with him or her. Self-medication must be avoided. When a person develops health consciousness, one is able to understand one's problems and seek solutions for them from the family doctor. Adopting a routine that includes eating correctly and on time, regular exercise, rest and sleep and following it religiously, will ensure good health.

Think it over...

When Swami Sivananda was asked what rules must be followed to maintain good health, he said, "Take Sattvic food. Drink pure water and breathe fresh air. Have sound sleep. Practise some physical exercises. Pray to the Lord and be cheerful. Worry not. Sing. Music also will help you much. Fast occasionally."

POINTS TO PONDER

1. Physical health is an important element of a magnetic personality.
2. People are known and judged by their habits.
3. Unless one has complete control over self, nothing can be achieved.
4. Do not try to become what you are not.
5. The human body is a master creation of God. Look after it.
6. Health consciousness is the foundation of good health and longevity.
7. A careful person is the best safety device.
8. Good health is dependent upon proper nutrition, fresh air and exercise.
9. Cleansing the body of waste matter is necessary for good health.
10. Relaxation helps relieve physical fatigue.
11. Sleep is a primary need of the human body. Do not skip it.
12. Make your family doctor a good friend.

Emotional Health

A magnetic personality is developed on a foundation provided by health and wellness. We have just seen why it is important to be physically fit, and also how it can be achieved. Nature has few demands, and if these are met, one can expect good health and a long life.

Just as it is important to be physically healthy and fit, it is imperative that one is also emotionally healthy to control and guide a fit body. This is important because emotional stress comes from almost anywhere. It grips a person through fatigue that cannot be got rid off through rest, relaxation or sleep. Modern medicine does provide short-term relief through drugs, but many of these drugs are habit-forming, and cannot be relied upon for long-term relief. When unattended, emotional stress leads to several physical ailments that could restrict the activities of any normal person.

A long-term solution lies in understanding how the central nervous system works in the human body, and also how one can learn to keep it healthy. While personal magnetism is manifested through the physical self, the real source of energy and power is the mind that controls the whole body. When the mind provides a positive direction to the body, and helps build good habits that support body functions, the individual emerges as a positive person. The personal magnetism is clearly visible.

THE MIND

You are whatever your mind has made you. It is responsible for what you are. Thoughts, feelings, attitudes and actions depend upon it. The mind can raise a person to great heights of glory, or drive the person to depression and a state of hopelessness.

The mind can achieve many things. It works like a processing unit in a computer. Only it is more efficient. Just as messages are broadcast from a radio station, the mind can also send and receive messages through telepathy. When the vibrations that emerge from it are in harmony with those of another person, both are automatically attracted towards each other. The similarity of the frequency of vibrations in two persons makes it possible. When the frequency is different, there is immediate repulsion. These vibrations affect personal relationships and also our possessions.

The vibrations that emerge from the mind could be positive or negative. These influence the people in the vicinity immediately. It is these vibrations that motivate people, either for good or bad. The influence depends upon the person from whom the vibrations have come. When the vibrations are positive, people strive to achieve more. However, when the vibrations are negative, people behave like a mob moved more by passions than by reason. Good people also behave irrationally when in a mob. The negative vibrations possess them until such time as their effect wears off, or is negated by positive influences.

The mind influences the personality of an individual. Everything gradually comes to harmony with the mind.

Success attracts success, and failure attracts defeat and dejection. The influence of the mind on life becomes obvious. The knowledge of the working of the mind can be a definite advantage. We can begin by understanding the difference between the conscious and the subconscious minds.

> **Think it over...**
>
> Look to your health; and if you have it, praise God and value it next to conscience; for health is the second blessing that we mortals are capable of, a blessing money can't buy.
>
> — *Izaak Walton*

THE CONSCIOUS MIND

The conscious mind is easy to understand. It consists of the five senses of sight, smell, sound, taste and touch. These senses are active when a person is awake and conscious. They put a person into immediate contact with the environment. All human experiences are based upon the messages received by these senses. These messages are conveyed to the subconscious mind for processing. In turn, the messages conveyed by the subconscious mind to the conscious mind are acted upon by the senses. The dual duty performed, the conscious mind is automatically switched off when a person goes to sleep.

THE SUBCONSCIOUS MIND

The subconscious mind plays an important role to shape the personality of a person. It has a vast potential to develop power within an individual. The subconscious mind, or the creative mind, as some prefer to call it, becomes active as soon as a child is born. It continues to function until death. The subconscious mind does not need rest. It coordinates and maintains the vital functions in the body. The messages received from the conscious mind are processed in the light of past knowledge and experience, and filed for future use, or rejected if found unnecessary.

The subconscious mind is a storehouse of knowledge and experience. It helps shape thoughts, actions, habits and attitudes. The feeling of well-being emerges from it. The conscious mind provides the initial experiences recorded in the subconscious mind. These experiences are deeply ingrained. Once stored there, they cannot be erased easily. This is what makes changing habits difficult. However, one can exercise control over them by altering the thoughts and actions to shape new habits, and eventually the attitudes. When a person accepts what is good, and rejects what is not, the subconscious mind generates creative power that promotes personal magnetism.

It is believed that experiences from the past lives, as brought by the soul, are stored at deeper levels in the subconscious mind. This level is also referred to as the unconscious mind. All the experiences are stored in the subconscious and the unconscious minds, and together they control the conscious mind. For example, on provocation, when the conscious mind is ready to hit a person, it is for the subconscious and the unconscious minds to immediately restrain it on the basis of past experiences, or to let it strike, create a new experience, and may be repent later. The subconscious and the unconscious minds could tell the conscious mind to observe patience and tolerance. While the conscious mind responds to logic, the activities of the subconscious mind are based upon selection and faith. Together the conscious and the subconscious minds can be valuable tools to bring about a change in the personality.

At a still deeper level in the subconscious mind we find what is known as supra-consciousness. At this level there is a great potential for creativity and power. All great men and women have been able to reach this level and tapped energy and power from cosmic intelligence. People like Swami Vivekanand, Aurobindo, Mahatma Gandhi and Mother Teresa were able to utilise this power. It is possible to reach these levels only through introspection, meditation and devotion.

CONTROLLING THE THOUGHTS

Everything begins with a thought. From the thought emerges a vision, and from vision an action. We are what our thoughts have made us. This may sound strange, but it is the truth. People often mistake wishing and thinking to be the same thing. A person might have wished for better things in life. Wishing is an admission that the person is not worthy of what he or she desires, and therefore seeks it through a heavenly miracle. To move ahead in life one must believe in one's ability. One can achieve only what a person believes he or she is worthy of attaining.

There is magic in believing. Whatever you believe, the mind conveys it to every cell in the body. Thoughts of good health, success and happiness benefit every part of the body. They also benefit those around you. When a person thinks of sickness, failure, hatred, greed and revenge, the thoughts affect the body, but in an adverse way.

Most people are not aware how thoughts can change their life. If you have not been able to benefit from this knowledge in the past, you can do so now. Visualize yourself, as you would want to be. Firmly believe in your ability to change. Do not wish for it. To wish for it would mean that you believe that you are incapable. It will not bring about good results.

To benefit from the fact that positive thoughts enhance personal power and negative thoughts reduce it, one must understand the difference between the two. A thought or action is positive when it is useful in a given situation, and negative if it is not.

With positive and productive thoughts the mind automatically generates positive magnetic vibrations. When the thoughts are negative, there is a corresponding loss of power. The personality depends upon the balance between the two. This makes the need for positive thinking obvious. Unfortunately, nineteen out of every twenty people lean towards the negative side of life. The figures may mislead people to believe that positive thinking is difficult to practice; otherwise why would so many people be negative-minded? However, this is not so. The plain truth is that people are not aware of the fact that positive thinking can benefit them.

It takes just as much effort to think positively as it does to think in negative terms. The difference lies in the attitude. Thoughts become actions and through repetition the actions become habits. These affect the attitudes and the environment, completing the cycle. The environment in which people live conditions them. With an overwhelming majority in the grip of negative thoughts, habits, and attitudes, the environment gets charged with a high level of negativity. The viscous circle goes on.

The environment continuously sends out signals or suggestions that could be either negative or positive in nature. The mind is on the receiving end. With a relatively higher incidence of negativism, the suggestions are predominantly negative. The magnitude of negative suggestions unfortunately compels the mind to accept them as correct.

Why not experiment to observe the influence of suggestions on a person? Plan so that four or five persons meet an individual at intervals, at different times of the day. Each time let the person point out that the individual is looking pale and run-down. Perhaps he needs to consult a doctor. By evening, the individual will really want to go to the doctor.

The positive aspects are equally effective. Have you observed that students score well in subjects when teachers suggest that the student has a natural aptitude for the subject? Similarly, an actor puts up a realistic effort when he is told that his acting is true to life. A soldier fights unmindful of the risk to his life when he believes that he is the best person to guard the frontiers of his country. Such suggestions and thoughts play an important part in the lives of all people.

It is not possible to control the suggestions that come our way from our surroundings. Therefore, it becomes necessary to control our receptivity to these suggestions, and also the thoughts that might arise from them. We should accept only those thoughts that benefit us, and reject the rest as useless. This may appear difficult or even impossible. However, it can be practised with a little effort. You must have observed that sometimes we fail to receive a message even though it was conveyed directly. This happens because of temporary absent-mindedness. In a similar way one can learn to deliberately close the gates of the mind, rejecting suggestions that appear negative and harmful. This way one can learn to screen all thoughts finding their way into the mind.

Here are a few observations about thoughts:

- All thoughts are important.
- Thoughts can be positive or negative. Positive thoughts release positive energy; negative thoughts release negative energy.
- Good thoughts are accepted hesitatingly. They are deep-rooted and backed by determination. They cannot be easily destroyed. They flourish in the company of good people.
- Bad thoughts are freely available and easily accepted. Many propagate them. When bad thoughts are avoided, evil and sin reduce proportionately.
- Thoughts are dynamic. They herald change for good or bad.
- Sow seeds of good thoughts. The plants will bear the fruits of good actions.

Think it over...

The secret of health for both mind and body is not to mourn for the past, nor to worry about the future, but to live the present moment wisely and earnestly.

— *The Buddha*

AUTOSUGGESTION

To enhance personal magnetism we can practice a positive version of what is popularly known as autosuggestion. One needs to understand it better. Everyone is already practicing autosuggestion. However, it is doing us more harm than good. We are feeding our minds with suggestions and thoughts that are negative. We fail to benefit from them. We only wish for more power but do not believe that we can develop it.

To make autosuggestion do wonders for you, believe that you are on your way to developing a magnetic personality. You must believe that you are moving towards greater personal success. You must believe that you stand for all that is best in life – truth, honesty and thoughtfulness for others. When these strong beliefs go deep within you through repetition of positive suggestions, observe how you feel. You will notice a marked change in your personality. The thoughts may appear small and trifling but they will emerge as constructive actions. These actions will forever become a part of you as habits.

AFFIRMATIONS

The use of affirmations is similar to the practice of autosuggestion. An affirmation is a firm statement that a person makes to the self. When the statement is made repeatedly, it influences the subconscious mind, and it becomes easier to bring about a change. Affirmations aim at helping to control one's thoughts, feelings and behaviour. While affirmations can be used to develop personal magnetism, many people have used them to get rid of problems like obesity, smoking and drinking. Many use affirmations to develop self-confidence.

HYPNOSIS

Hypnosis is the practice of causing a person to enter a state of consciousness in which they respond very readily to suggestions or commands. The word: hypnosis is derived from Greek *hupnos* meaning sleep. Hypnosis is an artificially induced state that resembles sleep. The person lies on a couch with eyes closed as in sleep unaware of the hypnotist sitting alongside, but the person responds to suggestions and commands.

Hypnosis is used to correct neurotic problems in an otherwise healthy person. These problems are usually attributed to undesirable memories in the subconscious mind. These memories may not be a part of a person's current life. They could have been brought by the soul from the past lives. For example, a person may have died in a car accident in one of the past lives. The soul may have brought the experience in the form of fear of travelling or speed, which cannot be related to anything in the current life. The problem may manifest in a serious form in the person's life. A capable hypnotist can cure such problems through suggestions during hypnosis.

Hypnosis is especially mentioned here because it clearly demonstrates the control the subconscious mind has over the human body, and also because the subconscious mind responds to the suggestions and commands given to it under hypnosis. These facts clearly point out that an individual's personality can be shaped through suggestions and commands to the subconscious mind.

CONTROLLING EMOTIONS AND FEELINGS

Through control of thoughts it becomes possible to control emotions and feelings. While an emotion refers to an instinctive feeling such as joy or anger, a feeling refers to the emotional aspect of a person's character such as feelings of love, sympathy, kindness, fear, anger, hatred, envy, and jealousy. A person's emotions and feelings influence the potential for developing personal magnetism. Like thoughts, emotions and feelings can either be positive or negative. They directly influence a person's health, professional success, family life, and position in society.

One should control emotions and feelings not only to develop personal magnetism, but also because of their distinct effect on physical wellness and longevity. While positive emotions and feelings of love, compassion and benevolence enhance the feeling of wellness, feelings of disgust, revenge and hatred keep one's wounds fresh in the mind. One may succeed in opening the lid off a person's darker side of the character by giving vent to these emotions, but the harm is twin-edged. It will have a detrimental effect upon one's personal power. Besides disturbing the balance of mind and physical functions of the body, the negative emotions and feelings rob energy and vital power. The loss is still greater when negative emotions continue to dominate one's thoughts, and through habit become a part of the person.

Emotions and feelings like greed, envy, jealousy and hatred are like invisible monsters, draining the body of vital energy and power. It is unfortunate that in most cases these emotions do not emerge from real situations, but only from imaginary thoughts. People worry about calamities that do not occur; they are envious, jealous and hateful without realizing that they are hurting no other person than their own self. The invisible monsters appear real because we have given them place in the mind. Each day they corrode into one's character, health and life.

If you are not convinced that these monsters are imaginary, write down on paper whatever torments you. Also write what could be the worst that could happen. Analyse the situation, writing the pros and the cons, just as you would write the assets and liabilities in a balance sheet. Discuss the problem on paper. It will immediately take the sting out of it. You will have the correct facts before you. You will know how and where you stand. Even when the worst is imminent, surely worry cannot avert it. Fretting and fuming can only reduce one's power to face the problem. Worry also reduces one's power to reason. When you have the problem sorted out on paper, go ahead and put the solution into action. One must look at the brighter side and ignore the dark one.

Encourage positive emotions and feelings of love, kindness, and sympathy for everyone. Love yourself; love your family, your work, and the people around you. What you give of yourself to others is added to you immediately. If somebody violates the faith you place in a person, forgive him or her because forgiveness will also give you strength.

Hatred and revenge will take it away. When the effect of positive emotions and feelings will begin to accumulate, you will experience the power they give you. Personal magnetism will emerge from within you.

> **Think it over...**
>
> Health is the greatest possession. Contentment is the greatest treasure. Confidence is the greatest friend. Non-being is the greatest joy.
>
> — *Lao Tzu*

THE MIND AND HEALTH

The mind plays a very important role in maintaining one's health. We all know how it helps maintain a fair balance in the functioning of the different systems that keep the body in good health. Doctors tell us that a very large number of ailments reported by patients are psychosomatic, meaning that these are the creation of the mind. These ailments do not have physical causes, but are manifested physically, compelling a person to consult a doctor. The doctor can prescribe only a temporary cure because the real cause and the cure lie in the mind of the patient. Unless the mental thoughts are corrected, the problem will persist.

Everyone would have observed a very common situation when a person is called to give a speech or make a presentation before a group of people. The fear of speaking or performing in public is one of the best-known fears known to mankind. Unless the person is used to speaking in public, we have a serious situation before us.

The person may experience a series of symptoms. The heart may beat faster, there may be shortness of breath, the hands and legs may tremble, the mind may go blank and the face turns pale. The mouth may turn dry; there may be an urgent need to visit the toilet. Many complain of an upset stomach. To the person all these symptoms are very real and distressing. The person becomes incapable of doing even the common everyday things. However, none of these symptoms have a physical cause like infection or disease. It is interesting to observe that these symptoms do not appear at the time of the speech or performance, but may appear several days earlier when the person experiences the threat of humiliation in the mind. The fear immediately creates the symptoms to help escape the situation.

Going by the symptoms, the doctors prescribe appropriate treatment. The relief is temporary. The patients may not understand that the cause of their ailment is in their mind, and may not disclose it to the doctor, who would normally go by symptoms expressed by the patient. Since this problem can recur again, many stage performers use drugs to calm down their anxiety, but that is not the right thing to do. The real treatment lies in the control of the thoughts.

The situation of a person asked to speak or perform in public is just one example. There are people who want to escape from a variety of situations in everyday life, and emotionally decide to escape it by getting sick. They may suffer a headache, an upset stomach, fever, fatigue, aches and pains and a whole lot of symptoms they can think of. The thoughts visualize the symptoms and the body executes the command faithfully. The person is ready to consult a doctor. The treatment may bring some relief but the symptoms are likely to continue until such time as the situation that created the need to escape from it persists.

Such situations are common when a husband brings along a friend for dinner unannounced, the in-laws arrive for a long stay, or the husband is a demanding kind of person. One may face a similar situation when the going is rough in the office, where the auditors are about to visit, or when one is not able to get along with the boss. When a person does not want to go out of station even if it were on a holiday, the mind provides the solution through thoughts commanding the body to create a variety of symptoms serving as escape routes.

What is unfortunate is that when a person repeatedly uses escape routes to face the realities of life, these become a habit. The temporary ailments take roots, and rather than disappear with medical treatment they become chronic, a permanent part of the individual. What started as an escape route becomes a cause for disease and decay. Such is the power of thoughts and the mind.

People who opt for these escape routes could have adopted a positive attitude towards the situation, and instead of giving negative commands to the body, they could have commanded the body to act brave, to act confident and to face the situation with the best of the abilities that were available. The situation would have passed through comfortably giving the individual added confidence and strength. This is very much like a person choosing between two roads. One may seem difficult but you know that it will take you to your destination. The other one is a short cut, but eventually you don't reach where you had to go. The person who seeks to develop personal magnetism follows a sure path, and adopts a positive attitude in life and keeps the mind and the thoughts well under control.

> **Think it over...**
>
> The way of a superior man is threefold: virtuous, he is free from anxieties; wise, he is free from perplexities; bold, he is free from fear.
>
> — *Confucius*

THE MIND AND LONGEVITY

Just as the mind and health are closely linked, so are the mind and longevity linked. We cannot totally ignore the genetic factors but there is ample evidence that persons with a positive attitude towards life live a long and healthy life. People who are in control of their mind, and the thoughts that emerge from there are known to have defeated disease and sickness, and established wellness for them.

At an early age, mother warned Bob that his father and grandfather had both been diabetic, and he must guard against it through a positive lifestyle. The mother's concern was well received, and Bob resolved to observe control over his diet and exercise. While he was particular about eating fruits and vegetables rather than starches and fats, he was equally careful to take a walk whenever he could. Even in his old age he preferred to walk a kilometer to post a letter at the post office rather than in the letterbox just a 100 meters away. The secret was in his understanding personal limitations and adopting a lifestyle that kept him active and healthy. He never got diabetic and lived a long life.

Old age is associated with several conditions like loss of memory, lack of coordination in movement, stiff joints, stubborn behaviour and many other similar conditions. A positive outlook can help people get over many of these conditions. These people appreciate that with age one cannot be as active as one is in younger years, and rather than complain about it, which most people do, they adapt the lifestyle to changing physical abilities. They change their food habits and activities to be in harmony with changing conditions. To keep their minds away from the little aches and pains that are a part of growing age, they keep the mind busy by participating in activities that would be in harmony with the circumstances.

Elderly people are known to have faced old age in many ways. There are instances like a lady in her sixties completing her Master's degree in English, persons acquiring new skills and abilities after retirement, and starting new ventures. Many elderly people regularly serve in social welfare organisations, using their lifetime experience to help build their communities. A large number of educated people turn to writing, and contribute their work regularly to newspapers and magazines. Many good books are the work of elderly people.

The number of elderly people is on the increase, as more people take control of their mind and body. These people can be seen living an active life, fending for their own needs, and even driving about in the chaotic traffic on the roads. A positive outlook, the result of a lifetime of positive thinking and an optimistic outlook, is helping elderly people to find a definite place in this vast world. They can look forward to live a purposeful life. In their case, one can say their personal magnetism has been put to the best use.

THE MIND AND ENVIRONMENT

We have seen how positive emotions and feelings generate personal power, adding on to one's abilities, health and life. The vibrations that emerge from individuals influence the people in the immediate vicinity. It is also accepted that people can communicate with each other over long distances through telepathy.

The power people exert over each other is clearly visible in places of prayer irrespective whether one is in a temple, a mosque, a church or a gurudwara. Since the people present are in a state of intense devotion, they generate positive vibrations that abound in these places. With an atmosphere of devotion and positive vibrations, the deity in the premises also becomes highly charged. Many people may not be devoted to the faith, but by being there experience a sense of joy that is typical of these surroundings. The feeling of joy lingers until it is neutralized in an altogether different environment.

Just as positive vibrations in the environment create a feeling of joy, negative vibrations in the environment create a feeling of fear. Everyone may not have had an opportunity to experience this fear first hand by being on the spot, but television has made it possible to witness and feel it from a distance. Have you ever carefully observed the negative reactions that spread around the world when the twin towers of the World Trade Centre in New York were brought down through terrorist attack?

Have you ever observed the negative reactions that followed terrorist bomb attacks in Mumbai, Delhi or London? Even without being personally involved people were awe-struck by fear and sat quietly at home thinking in prayer for the deceased and the injured.

The vibrations emerging from individuals do not only affect other people in the vicinity, but also affect our possessions and things. Have you ever observed why people consider some of their clothes lucky? You will see them wearing the same clothes on special occasions. Have you ever observed that people pray before they acquire a new vehicle, a scooter, motorcycle or car? They desire that it should be lucky for them. Through use they impart their personality to the vehicle. Everyday people pray in their shops, factories and business houses, desiring that good fortune should prevail. The vibrations emerging from the workers, the customers and visitors create their own influence on the premises.

Every home also enjoys a definite personality. This is the result of the influences exerted by the residents in the home. An observant person can immediately get to know how the people living in the home treat other people, their own possessions and things. Many people complain about the quality of products but little do they understand that a person's influence on the product is just as important as the quality offered by the manufacturers. It is all in the person's attitude. Have you observed that when you leave home for a crowded area if your mind tells you that you will find parking space, you will. When the mind says "no", you will fail to get that space. The mind is a wonderful tool ready to help everyone. It is for individuals to put it to correct use to enhance their personal magnetism and opportunities for success.

Think it over...

There is great beauty in going through life without anxiety or fear. Half our fears are baseless, and the other half discreditable.

— *Bovee*

FEAR

Many kinds of fears hold back individuals from attaining their full potential for a successful life. These fears emerge from the mind and create barriers that appear very difficult to cross. One needs to remember that the majority of the fears are imaginary. They are based only on a negative thought. When a person learns to control thoughts, controlling fears becomes easy. The secret lies in realising that fears are imaginary. Here is a list of 14 of the worst fears identified during a survey in U.S.A.:

- Speaking before a group
- Insects and bugs
- Deep water
- Death
- Loneliness
- Driving / riding a car
- Elevators
- Heights
- Financial problems
- Sickness
- Flying
- Dogs
- Darkness
- Escalators

Which of these fears makes you anxious? You are welcome to avoid situations you are not comfortable with. For example, nobody can compel you to go to a high place, or swim in deep water. In real life positions, as were discussed earlier, a careful person is the best safety device. You can rid yourself of financial problems by planning your money matters. You can avoid sickness by developing health consciousness. You can learn to speak in public or drive a car. The seeds of loneliness lie within you. Do not let them take root. When situations like darkness, elevators and escalators are to be faced, do it boldly. Millions do it everyday. Nothing unusual has been reported from anywhere in the world.

Everyone must learn to accept the truth about death. The day a person is born, the journey towards death begins. Each day gone by is one day less towards death. To get over a fear, do what makes you afraid. Nothing will happen. You will gradually acquire confidence. When individuals grow up and get opportunities to see death closely amongst the family and friends, they realise that death, the worst of all fears, is just a part of life and must be accepted as a reality and not something to be afraid of.

TRANSFORMING THE PERSONALITY

We have just seen how thoughts, words, emotions and feelings influence the human body in everyday life. These also influence the people in our vicinity and our possessions and things. Through these it is possible to transform the personality by feeding the correct inputs into the subconscious mind.

Experience has shown that while the subconscious mind responds to the words and everyday actions, it responds best to pictures and visuals. These provide a very motivating force to bring about transformation of the personality. Reactions to words are slow. Pictures create a deeper impact. They are easy to remember. They are stored deeper in the subconscious. Therefore, to bring about a swift transformation in the personality one must use visuals that are packed with actions. Together they will help transform you into a new magnetic personality.

POINTS TO PONDER

1. Emotional health is as important as physical health.
2. You are whatever your mind has made you.
3. All human resources are based upon messages received through the senses.
4. The subconscious mind plays an important role to shape the personality.
5. One must control the thoughts to give direction to life.
6. Autosuggestion can speed up the reconditioning of the subconscious mind.
7. Affirmations have a positive effect upon the subconscious mind.
8. A control over thoughts helps control feelings and emotions.
9. The mind can make or mar one's health. Many ailments are a creation of the mind.
10. Like health, the mind controls longevity.
11. The mind influences the people and objects that surround a person.
12. Many fears are responsible for robbing away the power to attract.
13. The personality is transformed through reconditioning of the subconscious mind.

Human Relationships

The most valuable skill a person can possess is the ability to get along well with people. Those who possess this ability are not only admired by their friends and colleagues, but achieve great heights of success in whatever field they decide to work. You will observe that people who occupy high positions are not there only because of their business and professional skills, but because of their ability to get along well with all kinds of people.

From morning until night everyone needs to deal with people. At home there is the spouse and children, the parents, uncles, aunts, nephews and nieces. At the workplace there are colleagues, the senior personnel and the subordinate staff. Besides, there are customers, clients and suppliers. Even in everyday life, besides the friends there are acquaintances in the organizations we belong to or visit, there is the liftman, the building guards, the gardener or the domestic help. In the marketplace there are shopkeepers, salesmen and shop assistants. Even the milkman, the laundryman and the postman who visit our home everyday develop a relationship that cannot be easily defined, but it exists all the same.

Success in business and professional life may be visible for all to see. However, this success is not possible unless we can develop relationships with people who contribute towards this success. The superstructure of success is built upon a foundation of good human relationships. Good people seek harmony with other good people, just as crooked people find satisfaction amongst others of their type.

The greatest leaders of all times were blessed with the ability to get along well with people. Those who were not strived harder. They observed people, and unraveled the mysteries of human behaviour. They strived to find what people desired before they could place their confidence and faith in others. The knowledge of good human relations is the result of keen observation and special perception to understand human behaviour. This knowledge cannot be passed on entirely to even the most dear ones. Everyone needs to learn and experience the intricacies of everyday human behaviour. A person who needs to develop personal magnetism must understand human relationships in greater depth.

RELATIONSHIPS BEGIN EARLY

Relationships begin to develop as soon as a child is conceived. In some faiths it is believed that a soul chooses the parents to suit what he or she desires to achieve in life. At birth a special bond develops between the child and the mother. This bond gradually extends to the father, and later to brothers, sisters and other people in the family. When other children visit, the child may develop relationships with them. At school there are all kinds of children and new bonds begin to develop. Many of them may last a lifetime.

It is believed that the first seven years in a child's life are particularly important in that many of the thoughts, attitudes and habits adopted in this period last through the lifetime. At this time much of the influence comes from the parents and the immediate family, and only partly from the teachers who teach in the initial years. All over the world the teaching responsibilities at this stage are entrusted to lady teachers because of their patience and tolerance, often described as the motherly touch. Psychologists confirm that the childhood influences affect the development of the personality of the child when he or she steps out into the adult world, very often only to be disillusioned.

The second seven years of a child's life may be a bit less important than the first period, but during this period every child undergoes major physical and emotional changes, which may be traumatic in some cases. At this stage the child enters adolescence and is exposed to different kinds of experiences both at home and in school. Some parents are overly protective. Most of them are not. However, the experiences, both good and bad, do contribute to give shape to the individual's personality, and the attitude towards adult relationships.

The best gift that parents can give their children is happy memories. No amount of money can buy these. Happy memories emerge from the parents sharing quality time, love and understanding with the children. The children must feel that the parents 'care'. Many of the bedtime stories that the parents may have narrated are repeated when these children change roles to become parents. When the parents instill a vision of hope and courage in the minds of children, they emerge as confident adults. Such a vision grows from experiences based on emotions like love, kindness, sympathy, generosity and thoughtfulness.

Responding to their experiences, people emerge as extroverts, meaning an outgoing, socially confident person; or as introverts, meaning a shy quiet person, who is interested more with personal thoughts and feelings rather than the outside world, or as ambiverts, meaning a person whose personality type is intermediate between extrovert and introvert. Depending upon personality types people build relationships at home, at workplace and community.

> **Think it over...**
>
> One must believe in marriage as in the immortality of the soul.
>
> — *Balzac*

RELATIONSHIPS AT HOME

While children grow up with strong relationships with the parents, as adults, the experiences with the opposite sex at school, college and otherwise, during dating or courtship, a significant relationship that emerges is that of a husband or wife. This relationship is the basis of the institution of marriage and the making of a home. It has withstood the test of time. Many alternatives have come and gone, but the relationship of a husband and wife holds its ground.

The day a person accepts a partner in marriage 'for better or for worse', a new life begins for the couple. Through this relationship each partner looks forward to mutual companionship, a happy home, and raising a family. These are not temporary needs. They must be met throughout life. Marriage provides a man and a woman a way to fulfil their natural needs.

With two persons living together intimately, a certain amount of stress is bound to build up. This gives rise to problems typical of a marital relationship. When one partner fails to fulfil his or her role as perceived by the other, conflicts emerge in the relationship. This necessitates that marital conflicts must be suitably resolved. The partners must appreciate the needs of the other and help find mutual fulfillment.

The institution of marriage is forever changing. At one time the man took on the role of an unquestioned master and guide. The woman followed, taking every word uttered by him to be the law. Today, marriage is a long-term partnership between a man and woman seeking happiness together. It is based on feelings of love, companionship and mutual welfare.

Generally, there is a freer selection of a partner. While the parents may still insist on satisfying themselves, yet there is every opportunity for a couple-to-be to meet and know each other before a relationship is finalized. This provides everyone an opportunity to know the other. However, human nature being what it is, there exist problems that makes marriage a gamble. The number of divorces is forever rising. These mean heartache for the couple, and also endanger the future of the children from such marriages.

It would be useful to appreciate the following observations about married life:

- Marriage is no bed of roses. The period of courtship and the first few weeks, or even months, of a marriage can be deceptive. They come and pass off like a pleasant dream, leaving behind sweet memories.

- Marriage is more than just a pleasant relationship between a man and woman. One must know the hopes, expectations and also the weaknesses of the partner. It appears easy to fulfil the needs of a partner, but they are more complex than one would think they are.
- Marriage is a difficult relationship because a man and woman are emotionally different. A woman may be physically weaker than man, but is endowed with greater inner strength and perseverance. Women are very sentimental about their perception of love. They seek affection not through sporadic expressions as a man's nature compels him to give, but in the form of little day-to-day gestures. While to a man the expression of love comes suddenly and flows out as rapidly, a woman looks forward to it in small doses all the time.
- A good marriage is based upon effective communication between the couple. When the communication breaks, problems raise their ugly heads.
- It is little acts of thoughtfulness for each other that strengthen a marriage. Each seeks the appreciation of the other. One must compliment each other as often as necessary. It must be done sincerely. It does not take long to detect hypocrisy.
- While to a man his success at the workplace is very important, to a woman her home is her haven. She seeks to express herself through her

home, and project the image of a happy contented family.

- The children must be the joint responsibility of the couple even though the wife may spend more time in shaping their lives. Their upbringing should be a united effort of the parents.
- The couple must have a clear understanding about family finances. Many women are now working and economically independent. This independence must contribute towards the happiness of the family.
- Family finances can become a serious problem when one of the partners is a spendthrift. Generally, financial problems arise when there is lack of communication and understanding.
- Togetherness is stimulating but everyone has a need for privacy. Both the partners must respect this need.
- The couple must respect each other's sentiments about birthdays and wedding anniversary. A gift is always a welcome surprise.
- Intimacy and sex play an important role in happy married life. It may take from a few months to years to acquire the art of physical love. Many learn it long after they are blessed with children. Some never learn it at all.
- Love and sex mean different things to the husband and the wife. To a man love and sex are the same thing. His emotions are active, forceful, rise swiftly, and wane as rapidly. A woman is different. To her sex means love. Her emotions are passive, re-

ceptive, and rise gently. This makes her feelings a constant challenge to the husband.

- A marriage can become difficult when a partner, usually the man, wants to dominate the relationship and uses aggressiveness to attain it. This attitude might have been accepted a few decades ago but is unacceptable in the present times. A woman can also be guilty of dominating married life, particularly when she comes from a richer family, may be more educated, or may be sharp with her tongue.
- When one of the partners is good looking, smart and attractive to the opposite sex, the problem of jealousy can ruin an otherwise good marriage. The problem exists more in the mind than in reality, but it must be tackled.
- Just as men can be rude and aggressive, many women indulge in nagging. Nagging literally means finding faults with trivial things. Most people consider it as a woman's weapon against man. When nagging assumes irritable levels it can endanger a good marriage.
- No marriage is free of marital quarrels. Minor quarrels can be helpful in keeping a marriage alive and happy. However, quarrels should not be allowed to grow. With communication lines open they can be tackled mutually.
- The success of a marriage depends upon the commitment of the couple to the relationship, and in accepting each other as individuals with personal hopes and aspirations that need to be fulfilled.

The relationships with other members in the family are equally important. Brothers and sisters grow up, get involved in a business or profession and make a home of their own. Yet it is important to maintain contact and relationships with them. In many cultures, families break up when one grows and moves out, but in the eastern cultures the family ties are strong, and individuals maintain contact and relationships. Experience has shown that this is a very positive way of life, and empowers one to face the problems of life.

> **Think it over...**
>
> The spirit of a person's life is ever shedding some power, just as a flower is steadily bestowing fragrance upon the air.
>
> —*T. Starr King*

PEOPLE AT THE WORKPLACE

The way a person gets along with people at the workplace not only influences one's personality, but also one's success. Whatever one may do for a living one will need to deal with people. There will be the need to deal with them as customers, clients or critics, and also as suppliers. The most important are those who work with us. Many may be working as subordinates. Some as colleagues. There will be many in higher positions. With almost one-fourth of life spent at the workplace, much of it in dealing with people, one cannot ignore the influence these relationships have on our personality and life. In the interests of personal success, it becomes necessary to understand relationships at the workplace in a little more detail.

RELATIONSHIP WITH SUBORDINATES

Irrespective of the position a person enjoys at the workplace, everyone seeks respect. The moment this respect is denied to him or her, the self-esteem suffers and the person denying this need is looked at with contempt.

A subordinate will hold a lower position than you, and may also enjoy lesser income and benefits, but that does not make him or her inferior to you. Provided the person has average intelligence and is given encouragement and guidance, he or she may be capable to rise to your position or even higher. Subordinates are human beings. They have a home and a family to support. Their needs are important to them. They deserve to be treated with respect, as one of the team.

Everyone is eager to rise in life. The promotion of the subordinates may depend upon your recommendations. Many of them will offer suggestions to enhance quality and productivity to impress you. This is their way of seeking your approval and appreciation. Many of the ideas that they offer may be useless. You might already have tried them. However, you will do well not to turn down suggestions without a fair hearing. Be patient. If you feel that a suggestion would not work, explain why. This way you will not kill the initiative of the person who might have worked hard to bring it to you. When people know that you respect and welcome new ideas, and will accept ones that are useful, they will strive to find those that are useful.

Your success depends upon the people working with you. To promote productivity, tell them what you expect of them. Also tell them how they benefit by becoming more productive. A person works more zealously for personal benefit than when the benefit goes to others.

The workers must be well motivated. They should look up to you as their leader, and not as one who passes orders. When dealing with subordinate staff at different levels, do not tackle those in subordinate positions yourself, but through those who are in charge of their work. Let everyone know that no job is too small for you, and that you are capable of doing even the trifling things. The working environments for the staff must be congenial. Advise them how to make the work interesting, and avoid monotony and fatigue.

Always express confidence in the workers. You can gradually delegate a part of your responsibilities to them. Let them make the minor decisions. This will give them a sense of involvement besides reducing the pressure of your work. This will also give you a chance to gauge their ability to take on assignments that involve more responsibility. When the workers get down to work, give them encouragement, appreciation and praise they are worthy of. If things go astray, as they will sometimes, do not hesitate to share the blame for their actions.

It is human to make mistakes. Accept them as part of work. Even when you know that the mistake could have been avoided if the worker had taken a little extra care, explain the shortcomings to him. This way he will continue to place his confidence in you, and accept you as a leader.

Lack of control over anger compels many to threaten an erratic worker with dire consequences. Do not let this happen. Rarely can these threats be carried out. Generally, a threat is given when a person is emotionally upset about a loss, and does not realize that it would not be possible to carry out the threat. Similarly, do not promise what you cannot deliver. To swallow one's threats and promises can be a very humiliating experience. You would also lose the confidence of a good worker.

A person in position is expected to be fair. One must be fair about distribution of work, about discipline at the workplace, and about promotions. Workers can be resentful about these matters. You cannot have preferences in handling situations. You need to be fair in handling complaints and breakdown of discipline. Be understanding, but firm. Take firm decisions. Be specific. Do not let anyone feel that you have varying standards for dealing with different workers. Let everyone enjoy your confidence, and place his or her faith in you. Do not demand respect from them. You must win it through your work.

DEALING WITH COLLEAGUES

Dealing with colleagues at the workplace should not present many problems. When everyone works independently there will be nothing to bother about. All that one may do is to be cordial, friendly and helpful. One can share mutual interests and ensure that there is harmony amongst everyone. When the activities are inter-linked and the productivity of one affects the rest, one will have to be careful not to let others down and upset the teamwork.

When a member of the team is inefficient and makes one link of the chain weak, it will require tact and patience to carry the person along. The team needs to realise that fretting and fuming cannot improve matters. It would be better to understand the person's problems, talk about them, suggest solutions, and help implement them. The senior management would already be aware of the situation. When things do not improve it may become necessary to refer the matter to them.

Colleagues do not appreciate when one of them tries to act superior in ability or intelligence. One could be better. Everyone may know about it. Yet nobody likes to accept the fact that others are superior. In such situations, rather than being helpful they may pull the person down in weaker moments. As a team member, one must contribute the best to the team. The senior management has an eye to spot capable workers. When they see one they will move the person a step ahead of others. When promoted, do not boast of your ability. Your colleagues think no less of their own abilities. You could tell them that luck has favoured you more than them.

Think it over...

I had rather do and not promise, than promise and not do.

— *A. Warwick*

DEALING WITH THE SENIOR MANAGEMENT

A person's growth at the workplace depends on how the immediate boss, or the senior management, looks at the abilities and performance of the individual. Therefore, one needs to keep the senior management satisfied. A few would try to seek promotions through the back door. They may resort to flattering the persons concerned, or by doing them certain out-of-the-way favours. Such methods appeal only to an unscrupulous few. In any business or professional organization, productivity and profits are important considerations. No activity in the workplace can be justified without them.

There is much that can be learnt from the senior management. It can be a great pleasure working with them. The immediate concern of a boss is how well a person shoulders responsibility to do the job well. To seek promotion one must know what is expected. The senior management is always focussed on increasing production and profits. They are aware that in any activity there will be problems, shortcomings, and even failures. However, they expect that a responsible person should be able to recognize the cause for such failings, and should be able to find reasonable solutions. Mistakes should not be repeated. Instead, each mistake should pave way for flawless working.

The senior management is observant and understands human problems well. They win the confidence of others quickly. Sometimes one may have to work with a difficult person. The person may be an expert in a specialized subject, but may lack understanding of human nature. Despite the hardship it may cause, deal amiably with such persons. Do not let his lack of understanding discourage you. When the boss hurls bitter criticism at you, do not respond with equal bitterness. Try to understand what he desires, and why. If you have failed to perform well, analyze the situation and tell him about it. Tact and patience are useful tools under such circumstances.

When your work is appreciated do not take the entire credit for your success. Share it with the entire staff. You will be rewarded for your modesty. Praise your efforts conservatively. When there is a problem or failure, step forward to take responsibility for it. Ensure that it does not repeat itself. Nobody likes a person who professes to be perfect, and blames others for shortcomings. Act reasonably. You will be accepted for what you are.

A quality that is appreciated by everyone is a person's desire to learn and perform better. When a person does a little more than what is expected, it is immediately understood that the person is capable of more responsibility — a hallmark of all senior personnel. The ability to analyze past failures, and to profit by the knowledge is another quality, which will promote you to higher positions in life.

Think it over...

We cannot live only for ourselves. A thousand fibers connect us with our fellow men; and along those fibers, as sympathetic threads, our actions run as causes, and they come back to us as effects.

— *Melville*

DEALING WITH PEOPLE IN EVERYDAY LIFE

Besides the people at home and the workplace one needs to deal with people in many other spheres everyday. The people one comes across in social life are no less important. Their opinions affect a person's position in society. To achieve harmony and goodwill with them, one should follow the guidelines for dealing with people. The usual courtesies must be extended to them. Every person is an individual in his or her own right. One responds with goodwill in proportion to the love and care one offers.

A genial temperament is an asset when dealing with people. Everyday we meet the lift attendant, the building guards, the gardener and our own domestic help. We cannot ignore taxi drivers, shop attendants and salesmen or the staff at clubs, restaurants and hotels that we visit. When you radiate happiness and goodwill, you get better service. Never look down upon those who serve you. Thank people every time they serve you. Expression of gratitude helps build goodwill. Accept special favours graciously. It is immaterial how small the service is. An attitude of gratitude is always appreciated. It promotes better service the next time.

PEOPLE AND STRESS

The initial contact with people is usually stimulating. It offers an opportunity to interact. However, the interaction soon leads to some anxiety, stress and eventually fatigue. The stress builds faster when dealing with some kinds of people. There are people who are fortunately insensitive to this kind of stress. They enjoy being with other people. Those who are extremely sensitive avoid dealing with people. Both kinds have their advantages and disadvantages. People make adjustments in life to attain maximum satisfaction. People avoid those whom they find stressful. This becomes necessary because stress is detrimental to health and can make life difficult.

People generally react to stress by getting irritated, fretting and fuming. This makes the situation worse. The solution lies in developing a positive attitude towards people. There is no such thing as a perfect person. We are not perfect. How can we expect others to be so? We need to learn to accept them as they are, and not as what we want them to be. It would be useful to learn why they behave as they do. What forces motivate them to good and bad actions? Can we take advantage of these influences? Perhaps we can if we can understand them better.

THE NEED FOR HARMONY

Nobody can do away with dealing with people. To be at peace, we need to learn to understand and cope with them. When we accept them as they are, we can find greater mental peace. The changed attitude would put an end to the conflicts that bother us everyday.

When a person learns to accept people as they are and recognizes those who have similar likes and dislikes, a greater possibility begins to take shape. We can take advantage of what Napoleon Hill, the author of Law of Success, has described as the principle of the mastermind. According to him, when two or more people are in harmony to achieve a common goal, then each person is endowed with a power that is more than what either of them could wield independently. This explains some of the greatest successes achieved by people in all spheres of life. Attaining harmony opens possibilities of success at home, at work, and in society. The ability to get along with people can become a vital force to develop self and others.

UNDERSTANDING PEOPLE

We should look at people from their point of view. Everyone considers himself or herself to be the most important person in the world. His or her name is the sweetest word that they like to hear. One wants to be accepted and treated as a unique person, the likes of which there never has been, or will ever be. Personal emotions and feelings are very important. These must be respected and honoured.

Everyone desires that the basic needs must be fulfilled. One desires to be healthy, have a home, a family, security of a livelihood, and a feeling of personal fulfilment. One likes to feel important and seeks appreciation for the good work being done. To every individual the personal problems are unique and nobody could face them better. Everyone has a personal philosophy about life. One will insist that it is the best and would emphasize it repeatedly.

On analysis one cannot help but agree with the individual. Every individual is the result of the interaction between the inherited characteristics and the environments in which the person grew up. Since no two human beings are born with similar characteristics, the need to be recognised as a unique person is justified and right. It would be all right if they hold different views. From their points of view they are right. Even when a person is wrong it appears right because that is how the person was taught. Coming from someone more knowledgeable it was accepted as the truth, and through repetition, it became a part of life.

Only one out of every twenty people looks at life from a positive viewpoint. Negative thoughts and feelings predominate in the lives of the other nineteen. The lives of the vast majority are ruled by fears of all descriptions – fear of criticism, of being ridiculed before others, of losing health, a loved one, or money, of failing in life, or death, and a whole lot of other things. Most people indulge in these fears unaware that they are imaginary, a creation of their thoughts.

People will emphatically refuse to admit that they have failed because they are negatively oriented. They will rationalize their actions, blaming their failures on other people and situations. Unwilling to change, they continue to live the life of a slave of invisible monsters. They have not known a life, which is free from such unnecessary worries, and they do not know what they are missing.

Think it over...

A word or a nod from the good has more weight, than the eloquent speeches of others.

— *Plutarch*

WINNING PEOPLE OVER

Before one can win people over it is necessary to make them feel wanted. Accept what is dear to them. Shower them with sincere appreciation. Remember their names. They have a home and a family like you. They need to feel secure and be appreciated for what they contribute to society. Take interest in them. Listen to what they wish to say. Respect their hopes and aspirations. This gives them confidence and self-esteem.

People seek listeners more than they seek advice. Lend a sympathetic ear. Speak sparingly but well. The way you speak is useful in winning people over. To be one of them, speak in their language. Unless you are speaking to learned people, do not speak in a language that sounds pedantic. When you act and speak in a superior way people feel ignorant and inferior. You cannot expect a person to appreciate you when you make him or her feel inferior. People are generally interested in many things. To be one of them you will need to speak their language and share similar interests. A person with a wide range of interests finds it easy to converse with others.

Avoid gossip. It has never done anybody any good. It usually starts with a stray remark about a person. When it is repeated it is passed on with a new slant. Soon it takes an ugly shape causing hurt. Negative criticism is equally bad. It repels people, not attract them. Before sitting on judgment visualize how you would have acted if you were in the other person's position.

Getting into an argument has never helped win friends. You may win the argument but will lose the friend. Do not give opinions or advice unless it is asked for. Remember, an opinion is just a suggestion, not an authoritative mandate. Even when you know that your suggestions are true and factual, leave acceptance to the choice of the person seeking your opinion. Do not be concerned about others more than what is necessary.

In dealing with people do not be selfish or insincere. The other person will see through them easily. Nobody appreciates insincerity and selfishness. Do not speak or act in a manner that your honour or integrity would be doubted. When defamatory facts about others come to your knowledge, bury them rather than repeat them. Repetition would be adding fuel to fire.

While you should be patient in hearing the woes of those who place their confidence in you, and advise them in as sincere and tactful a manner as you can manage, learn to keep your problems to yourself. People seek help from those who are self-sufficient, not from those who are in trouble. Radiate a positive atmosphere, not one of problems and gloom. People avoid those who brood and sulk. Smile. People will smile back at you. Laugh. People will laugh with you.

Optimism and enthusiasm are contagious. They make a person productive in day-to-day life and also help attract friends. People are attracted towards a person who is content. To make people like you, take interest in their welfare. Accept good time management as a part of daily life. Let people know that you care for their time. Let people know that you care for their feelings by extending simple courtesies like saying "thank you", "excuse me", "I beg your pardon" or "I'm sorry" in everyday life. These courtesies may appear trifling but they add a special charm to life, making a person more likeable. Complimenting others for their achievements is equally important. Personal success is important to everyone. Praise and appreciation help win over the toughest of people. People cannot help liking you when you like them.

ETHICS AND PEOPLE

There are shortcuts to winning people over but they are not right. Flattery is a common tool used to win people over. Many throw lavish parties and shower presents to attract the gullible few. They appear to achieve immediate success. However, such relationships do not last long. They are based on material benefits, and not on emotional bonds, which should form the basis of all lasting relationships.

To win people over on a long-term basis there is no substitute for sincerity, integrity and honourable conduct. A person with a noble character, one who is known for truthfulness and honesty, is accepted as a responsible citizen, one who is worthy of confidence. One should not expect immediate results with these virtues. People who matter in life recognize these virtues over a period of time. Relationships built upon a strong foundation are satisfying and lasting.

One builds goodwill by being thoughtful towards others. Kindness, sympathy and understanding, together with love add to the strength of one's character. Goodwill that emerges is a joy forever. When one enjoys the goodwill of people, one can be proud to possess the finest form of power that anyone can wield. When this power is used to benefit others, it grows. When used for self-appeasement it diminishes. Self-sufficiency is a great power-builder. All people look up to those who are so blessed.

Think it over...

There is a transcendent power in example. We reform others unconsciously, when we walk uprightly.

– *Mad. Swetchine*

THE ART OF CHANGING PEOPLE

It takes all types of people to make this world. Everyone grows up with an ideology as to what is right, and what is wrong. Many people would like to change others to their way of thought. However, the majority is not willing to change. With a negative attitude the vast majority sees no benefit from changing their way of life. People who desire to change others find it an uphill task. Instead, if a person were to change his or her attitudes towards people and accept them as they are, and not as one would want them to be, the world would become a more agreeable and happy place to live in.

People accept to change when they realise that a changed attitude towards life would bring them success and happiness. Making a change becomes easy when a person identifies better ways to fulfil personal desires. Success stories motivate people to change. Touching a person emotionally also encourages one to change. People are not receptive to new ideas all the time. Individual receptivity is governed by biorhythms. Therefore, suggestions for a change must be synchronized with a period of high receptivity. This makes it easier to attain one's purpose.

Generally, one should not insist that people should change. If it is necessary to bring about change, use the right tools – tact and patience. These virtues help one to get along well with people. When it is necessary to change a person, look out for issues where you and the person agree. Highlight the fact that both are in agreement on these issues. When both are in agreement, one could tactfully suggest the benefits of the proposed change. Fortify your statement with examples from your own life. This way the suggestion would be well received. Optimism and enthusiasm can help drive the point home faster. Your success can motivate others. People follow those who score goals in life.

FINDING HAPPINESS WITH PEOPLE

To every individual it is a personal challenge to get along well with people. People are fun for those who can get along well with them. With knowledge of what makes people tick, one can be successful at home, in business, or in society. However, do not go overboard with pleasing people. Nobody has ever succeeded in pleasing everyone. Personal happiness should not be sacrificed in making others happy. Live a balanced life that has a place for friends and companions. Be with people to enjoy the relationship, yet stay aloof to enjoy privacy. It is for you to keep your relationship with people congenial and satisfying.

POINTS TO PONDER

1. The ability to get along well with people is the most valuable skill a person can possess.
2. Relationships begin to develop early. Many last a lifetime.
3. Good relationships within the home contribute substantially to personal success and happiness.
4. One needs to maintain a variety of relationships at the workplace.
5. Good relationships in social life help to make life comfortable.
6. Contact with people is usually stimulating, but causes stress also.
7. Harmony within groups of people provides opportunity for success within the home, at the workplace and in the society.

8. People must be accepted as they are, and not as you would want them to be.
9. People will like you when you make them feel wanted.
10. To build good relationships there is no substitute for sincerity, integrity and honesty.
11. Do not try to change people. If you must, learn to agree with them on specific issues.
12. People can be a source of both joy and sorrow.

Etiquette and Manners

Everyone has to deal with a lot of people in everyday life. We meet them in our homes, at work and in the society. Every person is guided by personal needs and perception. Sometimes, these may not be in harmony with the needs of other people and may cause unnecessary tension and ill will. To overcome this situation people have adopted certain unwritten guidelines through customs and traditions. These help create harmony in human relationships.

These guidelines were not adopted in the form of a legal document. They have come into use through innumerable suggestions and refinements. The suggestions became actions, and through repetition actions became customs. These guidelines are not instinctive. Therefore, they need to be cultivated. They require a deliberate effort to learn and use in everyday life. These customs reflect good manners, and with usage transform into etiquette.

To develop harmony in relationships it is necessary to be thoughtful towards everyone. This comes from care and consideration for others. A thoughtful person always considers, "Is it fair to all concerned?" If the answer is "yes", the person goes ahead. If not, he changes his direction. Good etiquette and manners may appear trifling and insignificant to many. Yet experience shows that it is people with good etiquette and manners that move ahead. They are easily accepted everywhere.

COMMON COURTESIES

Everyone is taught four simple words in school. They are learnt but soon forgotten. Few realise their importance. The first word is 'please'. You may be using it, but never thought how useful it is. Just add 'please' to a sentence, and observe how quickly people respond. Every day, we say, "Can I have it?" In return we get average service. When we say, "Can I have it, please?" the response is faster. To our request, we have added politeness, a symbol of goodwill. Good service obviously follows.

We also learnt two simple words, "thank you". Generally, we use them on special occasions. We are shy of using them everyday. Say "thank you" to the little child who gives you a kiss; say it to your spouse for a little courtesy, or to the peon who brings the files to your table. They will appreciate it. You will be treated better. "Thank you" conveys sincere gratitude. It conveys appreciation for service. Everyone is eager to be appreciated.

Two other words that were taught to us in childhood but we find difficult to use are "I'm sorry". Most of us find it difficult to repeat these two simple words. It hurts the ego every time we use them. We were taught these words, but nobody told us that they could do wonders in our life. Whenever things go wrong, and there is the slightest chance that it could be due to you, just say, "I'm sorry". The problem will be sorted out. Initially it might hurt your ego. Soon you will realise that you have gained more than what you have lost. To accept one's fault is a sign of being a mature person. It is human to make mistakes. Why pretend to be God?

Another two words that can do wonders for you are "Excuse me". Wherever you go if you find that the passage to your goal is blocked, just say, "Excuse me". You will find that your way is clear. To make what we say convincing God blessed us with a smile. It costs nothing, but achieves much. Say it with a smile. See personal magnetism work.

ETIQUETTE OF GREETING PEOPLE

All over the world it is customary to greet people when you meet them. Some meet by saying, "Good morning" or "Hello", others may say "Namaste" or "Namaskar". Others prefer saying, "Ram Ramji" or "Jai Hari Krishna". Sikhs greet by saying, "Sat Shri Akal". Muslims say, "Aadabarz". Whatever be the form of greeting, it immediately removes barriers between people. It creates a feeling of oneness amongst them.

Some prefer to shake hands. Others join hands to say, "Namaskar." Some wave to say "Hi!" Some embrace. A few kiss on the cheek. Greeting each other brings people closer. It is a part of etiquette and good manners.

Greetings express thoughtfulness for another person. They make it easier for people to get along with others in everyday life. Greetings motivate. They inspire. They set a conversation going. They help develop friendships. Learn the art of greeting people wherever you go. You will be welcome everywhere.

Think it over...

Good manners and good morals are sworn friends and fast allies.

— *Bartol*

MAKING INTRODUCTIONS

On social occasions it is simple courtesy to introduce one person to another. Even when in a doubt whether they know each other, or have been introduced earlier, it will do no harm if you introduce them saying " I wonder if you have met...?" It would be in good taste, and a shy person will be at ease with others almost immediately.

There are certain rules about making introductions. Introduce a younger person to an older person, a gent to a lady, a subordinate to a senior, and a relative to an outsider. Some occasions may require minor changes. Make adjustments by combining the rules. While making introductions, do not hurry over it. Announce names clearly so that the other person can pick them easily. It may be useful to mention qualities of the person like " Please meet Sandra. She is a wonderful cook," or "This is Sam. He is a commercial artist with..." Such small remarks make for easy conversation amongst new friends. Everyone will appreciate your concern in making them comfortable.

DRESS ETIQUETTE

Clothes tell much about a person's tastes, and his or her likes and dislikes. Like personal charm, the clothes must delight the eye and the mind. They must be comfortable to wear, easy to care for, and elegant to look at. They must be suitable for the occasion.

At the workplace one must wear clothes that do not distract. One must dress conservatively. A shirt and pant is ideal for men. Neckties are optional in some offices. In winters, the woollen sweaters and pullovers should be sober. Not bright and gaudy. Lady employees also need to dress conservatively in office. Most prefer salwar-kamiz or sari. If used to wearing slacks, the tops must be long. Avoid low necklines or backless blouses. Jewellery should be restricted to the minimum, say, small earrings and a ring. A chain is optional. Nothing loud. Avoid heavy makeup and strong perfumes.

When attending formal functions at office or a social event, one must dress formally. Men can wear a formal suit with necktie. Ladies can wear heavier saris or salwar-kamiz for formal wear, and jewellery to match. Footwear is equally important. So are the accessories like handbags for ladies, particularly on formal occasions. Match them well.

When going to a funeral or condolence ceremony, it is customary to wear white, or light pastel shades. Avoid reds, maroons, pinks and dark colours. At all times, clothes must be attractive, not garish.

ETIQUETTE IN THE OFFICE

A business or professional organization operates from an office. Every office has a definite purpose and maintains discipline. Some rules are written. Many are not. Those, which are not written, come within working style or customs adopted by the organization. These become a part of office etiquette.

One-third of the working life is spent at the workplace. The etiquette we follow reflects in everyday life. One is accepted in harmony with the image one projects. One may only be a small part of a team. Good etiquette and manners contribute to make an office a congenial place to work. One can follow these simple guidelines:

- Time is an essential part of office discipline. One must fulfil responsibilities pertaining to it.

- Every office adopts a dress code. Follow it. It is not expected that men will come to office wearing jeans and tee shirts. Similarly, low-neck blouses and mini skirts worn by lady employees will not be appreciated.
- Every office has a working culture pertaining to handling of documents, files, office equipment and stationery. It is necessary that every evening the table is clear, the documents have been filed and files have been placed in the cabinets. The stationery must be back in the table drawer.
- Some offices serve midday tea or coffee. Many do not. This is not an occasion for a little chat.
- An office may provide one or more toilets. Leave the toilet in a condition that you would like to find it when you want to use it.
- In any office it will be necessary to deal with many people having different temperaments. Observe self-restraint and patience in dealing with people. Tact and patience can be useful tools.
- The telephone in an office is likely to be misused. The management never likes the office telephones to be used for personal business. It is good etiquette not to use the phone for outgoing calls without permission. Incoming calls should be received for an urgent message, and not on routine basis. Do not forget that when a telephone is used for personal use, it is not available for office use.
- Do not misuse office time. You are being paid for it. When you use time for any other purpose than office work, you are stealing time. If you have urgent work, there are provisions for leave.

- Discipline also breaks down when employees misuse office equipment like calculators, typewriters, fax machines, computers, printers and Photostat machines. Office furniture is another item of abuse. Avoid this misuse.
- Everyone is not entitled to use office vehicles. Use them within limits you are entitled to. Similarly, entertainment allowances are strictly for professional use.
- When men and women work in the same office there must be courtesy and decency. Remember that everyone has a responsibility to fulfill. Personal and professional activities must not be mixed. Treat each other as a member of a team.
- Every office has a definite policy regarding working additional time. If lady employees need to stay late, they must be provided transport to return to their homes.

Think it over...

Good breeding consists in having no particular mark of any profession, but a general elegance of manners.

— Johnson

TELEPHONE ETIQUETTE

Perhaps nothing has connected as many people together as the telephone. Today, one can talk to people anywhere in the world. Earlier, few homes had telephones. Now homes have internal exchange systems that connect every room through a telephone. Business houses have a telephone on every desk. Documents are transmitted through fax machines connected to the telephone line. Internet connected through the telephone has brought the world to every home. It has become possible to send messages and pictures, and even chat with people around the world. A vast storehouse of knowledge is now available through the Internet.

These developments have made it necessary to maintain etiquette and good manners on the telephone. A conversation on the telephone can make you happy and refreshed. On another occasion, it may arouse anger and hostility. It depends upon how you handle telephone calls. Here are a few things you will find useful to remember:

- A telephone is a device. Understand how it works. Learn how to use keys like mute, pause, flash and redial. Read the telephone booklet. Use the facility to store telephone numbers.
- Understand how a telephone is given a number. For example, if your number is 271 1234, the exchange number is 271, and your number is 1234.
- Every city too has a number. For example, Delhi is 011, Mumbai is 022, Kolkata is 033 and Chennai is 044. This way, every city has its own code.
- A number also identifies every country. The number 91 identifies India.
- One must maintain a personal telephone directory to record the names and telephone numbers of the persons one usually needs to speak to.
- For emergency use, the numbers of the hospital, fire brigade, railway station, the bus terminal, po-

lice station and your personal doctor must be on record.

- Use the telephone when you need to. You must know whom you want to talk to, and what you want to convey.
- When you get the dialed number, immediately disclose your identity by saying, “I am John. Could I please speak to...?” This way you have immediately conveyed who you are, and whom you would like to speak to. If the person is available, he will come on line.
- When you dial a business number, the receptionist will greet you saying, “Good morning. This is ABC Ltd. Can I help you?” You could then disclose your identity and the person you would like to speak to. If you desire some information, the receptionist would connect you with the appropriate person.
- If the person is not available, the receptionist will request you to call later, or leave your number.
- When an answering machine is connected to the telephone, you may hear a voice saying, “This is John Braganza’s residence. We are not home. Could you please leave your message?” At this point you could just say, “I am Joan calling. Could you please ring me at 323 1234? Thank you.”
- When you dial a number from a place where a private exchange is installed, as in some homes, in offices and hotels, you will first need to dial a number like ‘0’ or ‘9’, or even some other number before you hear the dial tone. Inquire the number from the owner of the phone. In hotels it is noted in

the directory of services provided in every room.

- Telephones at railway stations and airports may be connected to a computer. Follow instructions to obtain the desired information.
- When you order food or groceries on the telephone, identify yourself, the address and the telephone number you are speaking from. To ensure that it is not a hoax call by a prankster, the service provider rings back immediately to confirm the name of the caller and the order.
- When dialing international numbers, it is good manners to check the time of the country where you wish to connect the call. It may be daytime here, but could be the middle of the night in the country of your call. You could disturb the person at an odd hour.
- When a fax number does not respond, dial the number and request that the fax machine may be switched on.
- When speaking on the phone it is your voice that creates an impression at the other end. Speak courteously. Be polite. Answer the call gently. Never use harsh language. While speaking on the phone never converse with others simultaneously. Modern telephone instruments are sensitive. They pick up voices from a distance. Sometimes it can create misunderstandings.
- Sometimes you may get a wrong number. Say "sorry" and close the call.
- Receptionists need to be careful about voice training. Their job depends upon it. Always speak with a smile. Let it show in your voice. Your style should

express an air of helpfulness. Kindness and courtesy reflect good etiquette. Your image will linger in the minds of people you talk to.

MOBILE PHONE ETIQUETTE

Mobile phones have changed the way people think and work. These have linked people in the remotest areas almost around the clock. This has made it necessary that people must observe good manners and etiquette when using mobile phones. Here are a few guidelines about using mobile phones:

- People subscribe to mobile phone service for personal convenience. You have no right to impose upon it. When you want to speak to a person first try the landline number. Dial the mobile phone number only in an emergency.
- When speaking on a mobile keep the conversation short and to the point. If the message is short, use SMS (short message service).
- Most mobile phone owners are guilty of disturbing people in restaurants, cinema halls, and public meetings. Avoid this.
- Everyday we hear phones ringing at the wrong places. It is good manners to keep the ringer off when you are in a public place.
- When you need to respond to a call in a public place, remember that speaking even in hushed tones can be disturbing to others. Excuse yourself; move to a place where you can speak without disturbing others.

Carrying a mobile phone is useful when you are away from home. You can be traced in case of an emergency.

You can call in case of need. However, it is dangerous to speak on a phone and drive at the same time. If it is urgent, and you need to speak, stop the car and speak.

E-MAIL ETIQUETTE

With computers reaching every home people now send e-mails rather than write letters. Even within offices, inter-office communications are through e-mail. This has cut down upon writing conventional memos and letters, but there is now the need to observe e-mail etiquette. It would be useful to follow these courtesies:

- Unless you check your mailbox everyday do not give your e-mail address to everyone. It makes no sense if mail is not responded to.
- When writing mail most people do away with conventional practices like using capital letters, ensuring grammatical correctness, using proper punctuation and similar usage. They use abbreviations to write messages quickly.
- Write short messages in small case. Using 'all capitals' in the message is like shouting. Use this only when you need to shout at the recipient.
- When sending attachments ensure that they are not large. They can choke the recipient's mailbox.
- Do not send any unsolicited mail. The recipient will not appreciate it.
- Do not pass e-mail addresses of your friends and acquaintances to others without their permission.
- Send mail only to concerned persons. Do not send copies to everyone you *think* would find the mail interesting.

- Do not indulge in creating chains, or forwarding chain mail. No one was ever blessed by luck or received money by sending mail. Additional mail increases Internet traffic, slows down the services and irritates the recipients.
- Do not open attached mail received from persons you do not known. Many people have lost valuable data through virus received in the mail.

> **Think it over...**
>
> Good manners are a part of good morals; and it is as much our duty as our interest to practise both.
>
> — *Hunter*

ETIQUETTE AT MEETINGS

All kinds of meetings are held every day. In terms of manpower these meetings cost large sums of money. Many of these meetings achieve nothing. When organizing or attending meetings remember the following:

- Is the meeting necessary? Many of them are not. When doubtful, do not have the meeting. A meeting must have a definite purpose to achieve.
- Has the meeting been properly announced? Have invitations been sent to all the participants? Has the agenda been circulated? Have physical arrangements been made for the meeting? All these are important considerations.
- Meetings must start and end on time. Lack of punctuality exemplifies disrespect for other people's

time. Discuss the agenda item-wise. All relevant material pertaining to the points of discussion must be available at the meeting.

- If there is a telephone in the room, disconnect it during the meeting. Request the participants to have their cell phones switched off.
- If refreshments are to be served, they must be served either before the meeting, or after it. There should be no interruptions during the meeting.
- The minutes of the meeting must be recorded. They can be circulated later.

ETIQUETTE AT PUBLIC MEETINGS

Everyone needs to attend public meetings, as part of the audience, or as a speaker, one to introduce the speaker, or to present a bouquet or a gift to the special guest. One could also be presiding over a public meeting. In each of these cases one needs to maintain good etiquette.

As a part of the audience one's responsibility is restricted to being a gracious guest. During the meeting one should not talk, use a mobile phone, or walk around disturbing others.

When presiding a meeting one's responsibilities begin before the meeting, and end when the guests have left. One must know the purpose of the meeting. Ensure that the physical arrangements are adequate. As president you will need to welcome special guests, and also brief them about the meeting. At the end, the president gives concluding remarks before the final vote of thanks.

When entrusted with the responsibility of introducing a guest speaker, or presenting a bouquet or a garland, be prepared for it with the biodata of the guest, or the bouquet or garland.

When invited to speak at a meeting, accept the assignment only if you have something special to say. Ask the organisers how long they expect you to speak. When speaking, keep within time. Water or refreshments should not be served during a speech. Handouts must be distributed after the speaker has finished speaking. It should be ensured that nobody disturbs the meeting with children running around, or the audience speaking amongst them.

Thanksgiving at the end should be short. The purpose of thanksgiving is to say "thank you" to the guest speaker, the audience and others. It should not be an analytical commentary on what the speaker has said. That would be rude.

ETIQUETTE ON THE ROAD

Everyone needs to use roads. A road is a public place for everyone to use. Pedestrians and all kinds of vehicles use roads. Some vehicles move slowly. Others move fast. The slower vehicles must move on the left side, and the faster ones on their right. In the interests of public safety many facilities have been devised. Many roads have been divided with a divider or a yellow line, and driving lanes have been painted. Traffic lights may control the movement of traffic. Speed breakers, zebra crossings, overhead bridges, or underground tunnels may be provided. Take advantage of these provisions. They are conveniences devised for public safety. Follow these simple guidelines for safety on the road:

- Be acquainted with traffic rules. Follow them faithfully. The best safety device is a careful person. Be careful yourself. Teach carefulness to your family.
- Walk cautiously on one side of the road. While crossing a road, first see the right side, and then the left side. Preferably cross at zebra crossings only.
- Maintain discipline on the road. Be polite to each other.
- The slower vehicles must move on the left, and the faster one on their right.
- Give way to traffic on the right. Avoid overtaking.
- Slow down when you approach a light. Even if it is green, do not speed up to pass through before it turns red. It may turn red before you reach it. You may not be able to brake in time. At a red light stand in the appropriate lane.
- Drive in your lane. One who zigzags is a potential risk to self and others.
- Do not speed in the town. Speed thrills. But speed also kills.
- Avoid driving close to buses and trucks. Allow sufficient place for buses to stop at designated bus stops.
- Drive slowly near schools, hospitals and through crowded markets and areas. Blow the horn when necessary.
- Do not play loud music in the car. You may enjoy it, but it can prevent you from hearing a horn or signal. Besides, it disturbs others.

- Do not drink and drive. Drinking affects one's perception of speed and space. It also slows down reactions in emergent conditions.
- Do not use cell phones while driving. This divides your attention. It can also affect your emotions. This can cause an accident.
- When driving a two-wheel vehicle, use a helmet. In a car, use seat belts. If children are with you, ensure that they are secure in their seats. They can fall off when the brake is pressed suddenly.
- Always be courteous on the road. Even if the other person is at fault, give him the benefit of doubt. Avoid getting angry on the road.

ETIQUETTE ON THE HIGHWAY

A highway is not like the roads within towns. While roads within the town join people and places together, a highway joins several villages, towns and cities together. Driving on the highway is different from driving within the city. The journey within the city is short. On a highway the journey is long. The city roads are over-crowded. A highway is not. People move fast on the highway. Here are a few guidelines to follow:

- Keep vehicle speed within control. Safety is important.
- Always drive on your side. Avoid over-taking, especially on bends.
- Slow down when passing through villages and small towns. Beware of children and village folk not conscious of highway traffic.
- Do not brake suddenly. You could be hit by the traffic following you. If you need to stop get off the

highway. Keep away from fast moving vehicles.

- Maintain discipline at closed railway crossings. Line up on your side. Do not overtake waiting vehicles. One wrong move and the others follow. When the gate opens, it will create confusion.
- Be extra careful when driving at night. Many trucks, tractor trolleys, and bullock carts move without a light. Many accidental deaths are due to this single cause.

> **Think it over...**
>
> Coolness and absence of heat and haste indicate fine qualities. A gentleman makes no noise; a lady is serene.
>
> — *Emerson*

PARKING ETIQUETTE

Irresponsible parking is a matter of public concern. Millions of people are put to discomfort and inconvenience everyday. Parking lots are provided in every town. They may be located at the railway station, the bus terminal, outside hospitals, hotels, schools, colleges, near markets, and other such places. At some places one needs to pay a nominal charge for the service. At other places the service may be free.

To maintain parking etiquette, one needs to ask oneself a simple question, "Will my vehicle obstruct someone's passage, and cause inconvenience?" If the answer is, "yes", you are parking in the wrong place. Besides public convenience one must also consider vehicle safety. Many places clearly indicate, "Parking at

Owner's Risk." This implies that the parking attendant is not responsible for damage to the vehicle.

One may ride a bicycle, another a scooter or motorcycle, and some a car. All need places to park their vehicles. Even public conveyances like *rickshaws,* taxis and buses need parking areas. However, nobody is entitled to cause inconvenience to others. For public convenience and safety certain areas are designated as "No Parking" areas or zones. Do not ignore these requests. Penalties can be imposed for breaking rules.

ETIQUETTE IN A RESTAURANT

It is usual for most people to eat out in a restaurant. Generally, on arrival the steward welcomes and suggests an appropriate table. At peak times, if the restaurant is overcrowded, the steward may request you to wait until a table is vacated. Please do not lose your "cool" on such an occasion. Here are a few guidelines to follow when visiting a restaurant:

- Most restaurants offer a la carte services. This means that you can choose the dishes from the menu card, and pay for each dish. Sometimes a buffet spread is also offered at a fixed price per person. You can eat as much as you like from the dishes spread out on the table.
- The steward will inquire if you would like to order a drink. If you like soup, order that first. You could order some snacks with the soup. If you do not want soup, you could proceed to order the whole meal. Most of the dishes in a restaurant are big. Generally, a joint order is placed, and dishes shared.

- It is customary for the waiter to lay the table while the order is prepared. He will also place salad, pickle, chutney and ketchup to be used with the meal. When the dishes are brought in, the waiter may offer to serve everyone. He could also leave the food on the table for everyone to help himself or herself.
- After assessing the quantity, if additional food is required, the additional order can be placed.
- If you wish to call the waiter during the meal catch the eye of the nearest waiter or steward. It is discourteous to shout for him.
- The napkin is placed on the lap. Depending on the kind of food, it can be eaten with a fork and knife, or a fork and a spoon. Items like *chapatti, naan*, bread, etc. that need to be eaten with the hand should be eaten that way.
- At the end of the meal the waiter will bring warm water in a bowl to rinse the hands. Wipe them dry with the napkin.
- In some cultures a crushed napkin is symbolic of a very enjoyable meal.
- During the meal, it is customary to place the cutlery with the tips of the fork and knife pointing at each other like the sides of the alphabet 'A'. On completing the meal, the cutlery is placed straight in the middle of the plate like the alphabet 'H'. The waiter will then clear the plate.
- The dessert is ordered after the meal. If your prefer coffee to a dessert, or want both, you could order accordingly.

- Once the meal is over you could ask the waiter for the bill. You can pay cash, or by credit card, if acceptable. It is desired that you should leave an appropriate tip for the waiter. Besides the tip, you could compliment the waiter for good service.
- If you are not pleased with the food or service, or with a particular dish, do not let go of your anger. Ask the waiter to call the steward. Pass your complaint to him in a businesslike manner.
- On your way out if the steward is at the door, you can just say, "Thank you" with a smile. Courtesy motivates everyone to serve well.

ETIQUETTE AT A CLUB

People get together in clubs to meet and share common interests like indoor or outdoor games. Most clubs also have bar and restaurant facilities. Only the members and their guests are entitled to use club facilities. Club members are bound by club rules, which are periodically amended to fulfil membership needs. A managing committee elected annually administers the club.

Most clubs have a card room, billiard room, table tennis, swimming pool, squash, and badminton and tennis courts. Clubs may also have a library and reading room. Besides these, there will be a bar and a restaurant. Some clubs have residential rooms for guests. There are separate sets of rules for the use of these facilities. Members will necessarily need to be guided by these rules.

One meets and interacts with a variety of people in a club. To ensure good etiquette and manners, follow the simple rules of getting along with people. To be likeable, be humble. Everyone appreciates humility. Do not show off. Do not act pompous. Behave well with the members and the staff. A club is a joint property. Follow club rules. When aggrieved about any service, talk to the appropriate person. If your complaint is not attended the matter could be referred to the managing committee.

USING PUBLIC TOILETS

Everybody needs to use public toilets. We find them everywhere – in the trains, at bus terminals, at airports, in parks, shopping plazas, restaurants and hotels. They are provided as a public convenience. Life would be difficult without them. Do we use them, as we should? Do we leave them clean and dry, as we would like to find them when we use them? Everyone wants to use them but not care for their upkeep.

Simple rules apply for the use of public toilets. Use the urinal and toilet seats properly. Flush after use. If there is shortage of water, lodge a complaint about it. After using soap leave it in a soap dish or in a dry place. Do not leave the tap flowing. Do not spill water around the toilet seat. When people enter with dirty shoes, it leaves the toilet muddy. If you use toilet paper, carry some with you. It is not available in all public toilets. A little consideration on your part can make these public places more comfortable for everyone.

Think it over...

Manners easily and rapidly mature into morals.

— *H. Mann*

ETIQUETTE IN PLACES OF PRAYER

Depending upon personal faith people visit different places of prayer - temples, mosques, gurudwaras, churches, and others. Many homes have a place devoted to prayer. There is an equally big variety of religious customs and rituals. They may range from religious ceremonies at the birth of a child to *mundan* or sacred thread ceremony, or to ceremonies at weddings, special remembrances and at death. Each occasion requires certain etiquette to be maintained.

Most people consider footwear unclean. It is not permitted in places of prayer. In many places, as in gurudwaras and mosques, it is mandatory that the head must be covered. Some use a turban, others a cap or scarf. One sits on the ground and should be appropriately dressed.

On most occasions your personal presence and attention may only be required. However, sometimes you may need to carry flowers, incense sticks, a coconut, sweets, and similar items for prayer. When in doubt, observe others. Look out for local customs and rituals. Follow others.

During the ceremony observe self-restraint and silence. Do not disturb the ceremony or others. If *prasad* is served, accept it in your right hand supported by the left hand. If *tilak* is applied, and you are not wearing a turban or cap, cover your head with the left hand.

When departing from a prayer meeting held in the memory of a deceased person, it is customary to meet the bereaved family with folded hands. Nothing need be said. Your expression should convey your sentiments.

ETIQUETTE WITH NEIGHBOURS

Neighbours can be your best friends – and sometimes enemies too! It all depends upon the kind of relationship you wish to build with them. Follow these simple guidelines for better relationship.

- Accept your neighbours as good people. Only when personal self-interest interferes that problems begin to surface.
- Mind your own business. Do not step on each other's toes. Good relationships will develop naturally.
- Share happiness and not problems with neighbours. If there are problems of common interest, sit together and discuss how they can be resolved.
- If something went wrong because of your fault, apologise. Saying "sorry" should come as easily as saying "thank you".
- Co-operate with each other. Do not compete for petty things. Protect each other's interests. When you do a good deed, the neighbours will reciprocate.
- Gossip does the worst damage to good relations. Avoid gossip. Avoid criticism.
- Look at relationships with a positive attitude. A neighbour should be a friend who lives next door.
- Good etiquette and manners strengthen relationships between neighbours.

ETIQUETTE OF EXCHANGING GIFTS

A gift is a token of thoughtfulness for a person. It gives happiness to both, one who gives it, and one who receives it. The custom of exchanging gifts suffers when people begin to assess and compare the value of a gift. The purpose is defeated when one feels that it is not appropriate. A gift is a token of thoughtfulness. It need not be something that a person needs. Many people do not need anything. Should they not be given a gift? A gift reminds an individual of the emotional bonds of the person who has given it.

When one carries a bouquet of flowers to a sick person, it is not because the sick person needs it. His immediate need is medicine and medical care. Flowers cheer up a person. They reflect the glory of God. Their fragrance lifts up the spirits. Can any of these qualities be evaluated with money?

One should give with pleasure. One should receive with grace. Think of the sentiments of the person who thought and carried a gift for you. Keep giving and taking of gifts at a level both can sustain. Gift-wrapping adds value to the gift. Do not skip on it – even if it is something for your wife or child. When you receive a gift, say "Thank you" with a smile.

Think it over...

Good manners are made up of petty sacrifices.

— *Emerson*

SMOKING ETIQUETTE

Smoking is prohibited in public places like airports and railway stations, cinema halls and theatres, in hospitals, libraries and several other places. It is also prohibited in public conveyances like trains and buses. Many business houses also prohibit smoking in their premises. There are specific reasons for these restrictions. All smokers must observe them.

When uncertain whether smoking is permitted, seek the permission of the persons in the vicinity. If smoking is permitted, it is simple courtesy to seek the permission of those accompanying you. Without your being aware of it a person could be allergic to smoke. Elderly people are especially sensitive to this issue. Use an ashtray when you smoke. Put off the stub when you stop smoking. Do not leave it lit.

DRINKING ETIQUETTE

Social drinking is on the increase amongst men and women. It is considered fashionable to host cocktail parties. Some drink moderately. They stay within limits. A few drink indiscriminately, and end up creating a nuisance for themselves and the hosts.

Why is it that some people can drink a lot, and yet remain sober? Some get tipsy even with small quantities. One must appreciate that alcohol is a drug. In small quantities it can be beneficial. Like other drugs, the sensitivity to alcohol varies from one person to another. It would be difficult to assess what quantity would be right for anyone.

Drinking etiquette requires that there should be no unpleasantness for hosts and companions. One should drink moderately. Unlike food that is digested and absorbed in the intestines, alcohol is absorbed in the stomach. Drink slowly, sipping rather than gulping the drink. Do not mix drinks. Sometimes they can have a bad effect. Alcohol is stimulating initially. When the quantity of alcohol increases in the blood it causes depression. This can cause a hangover the next morning. Do not let anybody force you to a drink. "One for the road" is a folly. You are drinking for pleasure. Do not let it become displeasure – for you and others!

POINTS TO PONDER

1. Observing etiquette and manners promotes harmony in personal relationships.
2. Simple courtesies taught in school enhance personal magnetism.
3. Greetings and introductions between people promote goodwill and better relationships.
4. Etiquette in the office promotes productivity and goodwill.
5. One must observe telephone and mobile etiquette.
6. Use email discriminatingly.
7. Meetings can help promote productivity, but can equally be a waste of time and effort.
8. When invited to a public meeting be prepared for your role.
9. Besides traffic rules one must observe courtesy on the road and highway.
10. Wrong parking can be a source of inconvenience and irritation for people.
11. Etiquette and manners attract good service in hotels, restaurants and clubs.
12. When using public toilets leave them in a condition you would like to find them for personal use.

13. Observe self-restraint and silence in places of prayer.
14. Always respect the neighbours and people in high positions.
15. Give a gift with pleasure, and receive one with grace.
16. Avoid smoking and drinking in public.

Developing Personal Magnetism

Moving from one step to another, learning about the essentials of developing a magnetic personality, the need for physical and emotional health, it is obvious that the people in our lives play a significant role in shaping our personalities. It is equally obvious that good relationships depend largely on observing etiquette and good manners. None of these can be learnt overnight. They need a deliberate effort. One needs to pursue the goals persistently to develop a magnetic personality.

You are already on your way to developing a new personality when you have understood what helps to shape our lives. The willingness to change is a difficult choice, but once this decision is taken, one can be confident that a major step towards personal development is made. New activities will gradually lead to good habits, and these would result in making one more attractive.

You would by now be aware of your strengths and weaknesses. While it would be useful to emphasize upon the strengths, it would be necessary to get over the weaknesses. Set definite goals. Personal development should be top priority in any schedule of activities. The goals must be realistic and time-bound. A Plan of Action must be in place to guide one to success. It would not be long before you will emerge as a confident person, ready to get ahead to achieve great things in life.

> **Think it over...**
>
> Man himself is the crowning wonder of creation; the study of his nature is the noblest study the world affords.
>
> — *Gladstone*

YOU ARE UNIQUE

One of the greatest mistakes people make in transforming their personalities is that they try to become what they are not. They fall an easy prey to copy some of the people they admire in their life. They forget that everyone is unique. Everyone is born with a different genetic setup. Everyone has been exposed to different environments. Each individual has grown with different thoughts and perceptions. Under such circumstances how can two people be alike? When one copies another, the originality is lost. One becomes a 'copy'. A copy is proof of the original, but never receives or attracts the importance of the original.

It has repeatedly been emphasized that you are unique. Millions of people have come to this world and gone, but none of them was like you. You are surrounded by millions of people living today, but none of them is like you. Even the people who have yet to come to this world will never be like you. Why should you then try to become like anyone of them? Maintain your originality. Do not copy others. If you need to copy, it should not be their personality as a whole, but their strengths or virtues that contribute to make them attractive to you. Virtues like truthfulness, honesty, sincerity, kindness and benevolence need to be made a part of our lives.

Many people contend that these virtues are difficult to live with in the modern world of cutthroat competition. Yet we see them practised by many successful people. If one must copy, then one must copy how these individuals have been able to create a balance between virtues and a successful life. Success without virtues is always short-lived. Lives of people who attained great heights only to come down too soon have proved this fact repeatedly.

WHAT IS YOUR SPECIALTY?

Have you ever noticed how many products are known by their qualities? For example, Lux is internationally known as the soap for beautiful people. Surf and Ariel are known as detergents that help easy laundering of dirty clothes. Every business-house is out to create an image for their products – a brand image. Each brand is known for a particular quality, a specialty. This creates a demand for the product not only at the local or national level, but also in other parts of the world.

In the same way, people are known for their qualities. People are often identified for their being truthful, honest and reliable. Mahatma Gandhi was known for preaching non-violence. He will always be remembered for that. Mother Teresa was known for her service to the destitute. She will always be remembered for that. Many people are also known for their negative image. Hitler was known as a ruthless dictator. People are also known to be cheats, dishonest and unreliable.

What is your specialty? How would you like people to label you? What kind of an image would you like to project? What virtues are your strengths? Are there any negative qualities that are hard to overcome, and you wish to camouflage? As an individual, everyone must decide the kind of person one would like to be, and also known by that image. That would be your 'brand' image. You will need to develop it gradually.

To succeed follow these simple guidelines:

- Be what you are. Identify what you want to be. Know what makes you unique.
- Do the things you like to do. Know what you can do best. Repeat your successes.
- Use your talents and blessings to help others. Touch people in a meaningful way. They will always remember you for your concern.
- Have a life, not a lifestyle. Do what makes you happy. Be with people who matter.

THE PACKAGING

In the modern world packaging plays as important a role as the product itself. The packaging not only protects the product when it moves from the factory to the consumer through wholesalers and retailers, but also adds to making it more attractive to the consumer. The packaging needs to be attractive to arouse interest and desire for the product. Most consumers do not immediately require the products they buy. It is the packaging that compels them to pick and examine a product in a store. When the desire for the product is aroused, it ends with yet another sale. Gifts are often so attractively packed that one hesitates to undo the wrapping. The outer wrapping enhances the excitement for the gift.

The clothes people wear can be compared to the packaging of products. The style of dress draws immediate attention. Many people are known by particular styles in clothes. Most people are conservative. They will stick to established patterns of dress, wearing the usual designs and colours that they have known within the family and amongst the people they move with. A few experiment with new designs. Some are even obsessed with changing styles and desire to wear exclusive designs.

Different occasions demand different types of clothing. At home one desires to be comfortable and casual. Both men and women go to work. The clothes need to be decent and practical. Many companies have set dressing etiquette, and this needs to be maintained. On social occasions it is customary to wear one's best. Accessories add on to make one look special.

Most people tend to overdo. It becomes too obvious that they are 'showing off'. Rather than make them look attractive, an overdone style creates a negative image. Therefore, moderation is important in matters of dress and clothing. The clothes must be practical, comfortable and yet be attractive. With changing styles and the desire to adopt them, it would be wrong to prescribe rules for dressing appropriately, but it is important that one should not look odd or out of place. One must dress to suit the occasion and the environment.

> **Think it over...**
>
> Men are not to be judged by their looks, habits and appearances; but by the character of their lives and conversations, and by their work. 'Tis better that a man's own work than that another man's words should praise him.
>
> — *L'Estrange*

BODY SIGNALS

Though most people are unaware of it, thoughts and emotions are continuously being communicated through body gestures, referred to as 'body language'. Confidence, an essential element of a magnetic personality, is reflected by the way a person stands, walks, sits and acts in the normal course of everyday life. One should not forget that an individual is a combination of several identifiable activities that together contribute to the development of personal magnetism.

Biorhythms refer to a recurring cycle in the functioning of an organism, such as the daily cycle of keeping awake and sleeping. It cannot be overlooked that as time flows we experience a day and a night. Over a longer period we experience the changes in weather and climates, which affect human beings and also the plant and animal life. We need to understand that biorhythms influence every individual. This influence has a direct effect upon the personality and personal efficiency. One is more efficient and attractive at one time, and not as much on other occasions. An understanding of personal biorhythmic activity can help a person project a positive image in everyday life.

Communication through spoken words is an important factor that influences personal charm. Therefore, one must try to cultivate a pleasant and rhythmic voice. We know how good public speakers are able to hold the attention of the audience. They were not born with speaking skills. They acquired them through training and personal effort.

In everyday life one must learn to be a good conversationalist. This becomes easy when a person takes interest in people. Self-education should be a part of the daily routine. Stimulate your thinking through study, travelling, and meeting and learning about people. The more one knows the better one can impress the people. Speak well of people. If you cannot, it is better not to speak at all. Unpleasant facts about others are best forgotten, rather than repeated.

DEVELOPING PERSONAL POWER

All human beings are basically selfish. To them their needs are most important. When their basic needs are fulfilled, they strive to exert power over others. Since everyone is pursuing this need, the struggle for power creates differences and conflicts amongst people. The person who wants to get ahead and be acknowledged by others in life must maintain good relations with as many people as possible. This makes it necessary for the person to understand how individuals seek to enhance personal power.

The show of physical strength is the most primitive form of power. To the primitive man, might was right. It is the same for many people even today. However, in a civilized society the concept of physical strength has changed substantially. People look forward to it as good health, and as an ability to participate in a variety of activities, games and sports. Boxing, wrestling, weightlifting, javelin and discus throw and several other games are examples of the intelligent use of physical strength as a source of power. The brutal use of physical strength is best left to the unscrupulous few, and to the police and military personnel who are responsible to maintain law and order in a civilized society.

With limitations to the use of physical strength as power, mankind devised yet another form of power – knowledge! When a person knows more than others about any subject, it means power. This has motivated people to learn a variety of skills, to gaining knowledge about the mysteries of nature, and by gaining experience to tackle difficult situations. This has made it possible for people to gain specialised knowledge in every sphere of life. This has also promoted technological growth and knowledge, ensuring a better living for people all over the world. Knowledge is best gained through education, through study and experience. While the desire for power through knowledge has promoted specialization, it has narrowed the perception of individuals. To live a complete life one needs to be knowledgeable about many facets of life.

With many people striving to gain knowledge as a form of power, the obvious result is one person holding a position that is more conspicuous than others. The holding of important positions has motivated people to work harder, rise higher in business and professions, and gain positions in organizations through goodwill and influence. The desire to project a position of importance people build and live in houses that are much larger than what they require. They acquire objects to show off. They possess more of status symbols than objects of personal need. A certain amount of responsibility is attached to every position. One is able to maintain the position as long as one fulfils the responsibilities that go with the position. When a person fails to fulfil the responsibilities one automatically slides to a position one is worthy of. One cannot possibly hold a position forever. With the loss of position the influence is automatically altered.

In the modern world one of the most conspicuous forms of power that people wield is the power that comes from money. Besides being used to buy the necessities and luxuries of life, money is often used to shower gifts and charity to impress others. It is money that labels individuals and nations as rich or poor. The true worth of money lies in the way it is used. In the hands of good people much good can be attained with money. It can be the stepping-stone to progress and wealth. However, the possession of money does not mean that it has been rightfully or personally earned. It could be inherited, borrowed or acquired unethically. To the intelligent person money is a good slave, but a poor master.

The best source of power is human goodwill. This source of power can do wonders irrespective of whether one is rich or poor, physically strong or weak, belongs to an exclusive group of people in high positions or is one of the ordinary lot. This power emerges from a positive outlook towards people. It develops from simple little acts of kindness – a smile, a little encouragement, replacing despair with hope. It is a simple art of adjusting with and liking all people. It can begin from the home, and be extended to the friends, at the workplace and in the society.

People who believe in human goodwill as a source of power benefit others as much as they benefit themselves through a magnetic personality.

THE POWER FROM WITHIN

It is easier to understand and adopt the external factors that help attract immediate attention. However, beyond helping in drawing attention, they cannot promote personal magnetism. To be truly attractive one needs to draw from resources lying latent deep within each one of us. Irrespective of one's external characteristics, everyone is endowed with this inner power, which can be developed to work wonders. Once this power is developed, it becomes a part of the individual. It can be effortlessly used to influence the people one comes across everyday.

This power has distinguished all great men. One does not need to do great things to develop it for personal benefit. To acquire it, it is as simple as making important little things a part of the daily life. It is the small things well done that help develop the personality. Let us now see how these important factors affect us everyday, and what we can do to make them a part of us.

Think it over...

Actions, looks, words, steps, form the alphabet by which you may spell characters: some are mere letters, some contain entire words, lines, pages, which at once decipher the life of a man. One such genuine uninterrupted page may be your key to all the rest; but first be certain that he wrote it all alone, and without thinking of publisher or reader.

— *Lavater*

CHARACTER

If we were to search for a single factor that promotes personal magnetism, the answer would simply be: our character. It makes us unique. It is a valuable possession. Its strength knows no boundaries of colour, caste or creed. The financial status has no bearing on it either. It is such a potent power that when developed in its noblest form, it knows no limitations. It easily overshadows the possession of riches, knowledge, intellect, or genius. All great people have distinguished themselves through their character.

A person's character represents what he or she believes in. It can take a person to great heights of glory and admiration, almost in line with the gods. The character helps to bring out and project the virtues in a person. When the development of the character is neglected, it can lead to falling into a well of loneliness, further leading one to failure and even ruin.

To develop personal power through one's character means to learn to be dutiful, conscientious, truthful and honest. All the religions also aim to teach us the same thing. To be convincing, the simple truth is written in many forms, and illustrated with lives of men and women who were perhaps no different from what we are today.

When one accepts the principles of truthfulness, honesty and thoughtfulness towards others, and makes them a part of everyday life, one adds on a very vital force. This force has identified all great men and women who became immortal through their thoughts and actions. This force can enhance the magnetic influence of a person over a very large area.

A person's character is not reflected through a single act of great intelligence, genius, or greatness. It is made of little, seemingly insignificant actions in everyday life. Every fleeting thought affects it. Thoughts become actions, and actions turn into habits. The laws of action and reaction influence every little action a person performs. We may not be aware of it, but all good and bad deeds are either rewarded or punished. In some cases the results become apparent immediately. Sometimes they are not. Even then the points are scored in favour or against immediately.

The development of character in its noblest form offers unlimited rewards. It adds new dimensions to a person's life. The person with 'character' stands out in society. As with all good things in life, before it can be achieved, there are always hurdles to cross, many temptations to be avoided. However, there is nothing that a person cannot achieve through determination and effort. It will lead to recognition and admiration. Through development of character a great power that will always be at your service will be added on to you. With it you will experience happiness that you have never known before.

THE VOICE WITHIN

Many faiths teach that God resides within each one of us. We cannot see Him just as we cannot see our own image in a mirror covered with dust. Over several births we have gradually ignored virtues like patience, tolerance, kindness and benevolence that can be identified with God. Instead we have indulged in impatience, greed, anger and hatred, the very qualities God desires us to forsake. Can we then communicate with Him?

To experience the power from God begin simply by thanking Him for all that He has blessed you with. A man used to curse God every day for not giving him enough money to buy a new pair of shoes until one day he met a man who had no legs. Unfortunately, we take most of the gifts from God as granted. We forget that he has blessed us with two eyes, two ears, two arms, two legs, and above all a healthy body and a mind, the ability to live well and think good thoughts with. We find it easier to think of what we do not have, and never of what we do have.

We seek God in temples, mosques and churches. We seek Him in places of pilgrimage. We forget that He resides within each of us, waiting for us to talk to Him, to seek His guidance and live a life of happiness. All He asks of us is to live a simple life built upon virtues, and avoid actions that hurt others and us. God resides within us as our conscience. It is often repeated, "Whenever in doubt, seek the answer from within you. You will get the right answer." God speaks to us through our conscience. We shape the conscience with our character.

> **Think it over...**
>
> Your body is the temple of the Holy Spirit, which is in you, which ye have of God: therefore glorify God in your body.
>
> — *Corinthians*

SPEAKING TO GOD

When we talk to God in the form of little prayers thanking Him for all the blessings, we begin to enjoy our conversations with Him. Not only are our problems solved, but we also experience a new kind of peace. In accepting and talking to Him, we heal our inner-self through meditation.

To meditate means to think fully and deeply – about our self. The word: meditation is derived from the Latin root meaning, "to heal". The more we meditate, the better we feel. Through meditation, we begin to understand the futility of our desires, of our greed and ignorance. As we avoid them, we heal our inner-self. It is a personal experience beyond comparison. Gradually it takes us deeper into the inner-self. In silence, we introspect about our thoughts and feelings, about what we experience in our life. In silence, we realize our identity with the great power that guides and protects us.

When we go deeper, we begin to see the attributes of God through prayer and meditation. We feel the peace, the patience, tolerance, love and goodwill. We begin to see life with a new perspective. Life becomes a new and better experience. We stop seeking happiness that comes from material possessions, but rather seek it from within.

Prayer is simply talking to God. Many seek the guidance and support of a teacher or a guru to learn meditation. If you have not found a guru, you need not be deprived from the happiness of meditation. Choose a time that is convenient to you, preferably in the morning. Find a quiet corner, away from interruptions like the telephone. Sit comfortably on a mat or cushion on the floor, cross-legged with your hands resting comfortably in the lap. If you find sitting on the floor difficult, you could sit on a chair with your legs resting on the floor, and hands on your lap.

Keep the back straight. An upright spine helps the energy flow up and down.

Take a few deep breaths. Closing your eyes gently, think of God. He is formless. Yet we look at Him in a form that is in harmony with our thoughts. We know Him in many forms as Ram, Krishna, Christ, Mahavir, Allah or Buddha. Think of Him in whatever form you like. Repeat His name in reverence. Repeatedly surrender your actions to Him. Visualize that as a child you have His attributes – inner peace, tolerance, kindness and love. Thank Him for these qualities. Day after day, as you repeatedly meditate, your craving for greater inner peace will grow. You will become a new person – confident, peaceful and happy. People will find you attractive.

THE POWER FROM SERVING OTHERS

Good and evil have existed on this earth since the very beginning. Whenever a person performed good actions, he or she benefits from it in many ways. In the same way when a person indulges in bad or selfish actions, which bring temporary pleasure, ultimately evil always boomerangs on the individual who indulges in it, and may even bring about destruction.

Have you ever watched how a boxer keeps punching a bag with all his strength and vigour? Doesn't it look foolish? A person hitting a lifeless bag like a mad man? The boxer has a reason. He knows that with each punch he is gaining an equal amount of power within his arm to prepare for the bout on the great day. Similarly, when a person does a good act by helping someone in need, the satisfaction of having reduced some discomfort or distress in the world enhances personal power in equal measure.

At the workplace everyone is aware that better service translates into greater power in the form of money. The social worker does not derive power in the form of money, but in the form of enhanced magnetism in the personality. This simple fact motivates people to devote a part of their time to serve, to reduce distress and suffering. This fact has also motivated the rich to give huge charities for good causes. When a person gives a part of oneself to serve the needy, it comes back manifold to develop a magnetic personality.

When you smile at a person you get back a smile in return. When you are thoughtful about a person you immediately build goodwill. When you help the needy, distressed and the suffering, you get gratitude. At the same time a powerful force develops within you. When you do good actions you are really multiplying your personal power. This way your influence will grow, initially over a few, but gradually over a large area in your community and elsewhere. This new power will bring you happiness, good health, and a long life when you shift attention from yourself to your family, the community and the country.

USING THE NEW POWER

When you become virtuous, you begin to experience a new kind of magnetism from within you. You develop a special instinct, an intuition, or a sixth sense, as some prefer to call it. This sixth sense guides a person through a better understanding of what is happening or is about to happen. It is indeed a powerful force, and sets people wondering with its many miracles. It is a power that puts a person in touch with nature's storehouse of knowledge and power. One can draw from it continuously for the progress of mankind. Experience has confirmed that when this power is used for the benefit of mankind, it grows. On the other hand, if used for wrong purposes, or for gaining undue advantage over the weak, this power begins to wane. It is for you to decide what use you wish to use your new power, the power of a magnetic personality.

POINTS TO PONDER

1. You are unique. Do not try to be someone else.
2. Every individual must be known for his or her qualities just as products are known by brand names.
3. Clothes are to individuals what packaging is to products.
4. A person's personality is judged by the level of confidence reflected through body language.
5. Mankind is forever in search of ways to develop and exert personal power in many ways.
6. Every person has a storehouse of power lying latent waiting to be usefully tapped.
7. An individual's character represents what one believes in.
8. God is the greatest source of unfailing power. Learn to use it.
9. A virtuous life, prayer and meditation connect an individual with God.
10. God is easily pleased through service to the weak and the needy.
11. Personal magnetism is a great source of power. Always use it for the welfare of mankind.